Leaf Shadows and Sunshine

To
all the daughters who seek to
forgive and accept their mothers
and
all the mothers who seek to forgive themselves.

Leaf Shadows and Sunshine

Heather Starsong

This is a work of fiction. Names, characters, places and events described herein are products of the authors's imagination or are used fictitiously. Any resemblance to actual events, locations, organizations, or persons, living or dead, is entirely coincidental. The village of Woodborough is fictitious.

Leaf Shadows and Sunshine
Copyright © 2022 Heather Starsong (www.heatherstarsong.com)

All rights reserved. No part of this book may be used or reproduced in any manner whatsoever without written permission, except in the case of brief quotations embodied in critical articles or reviews.

Author: Heather Starsong
Title: *Leaf Shadows and Sunshine*

Cover art by Stephen Clay Elliott
Design and layout by Ann Erwin
Proofreading by Margaret Pevec

Description: First edition | Boulder, CO: Dancing Aspen Press
Identifiers: ISBN Trade Paperback #978-0-9975450-8-1
        ISBN eBook #978-0-9975450-9-8
Subjects: Fiction, Family Relationships, History, Women's Literature, Cats

Table of Contents

Chapter One	7
Chapter Two	29
Chapter Three	43
Chapter Four	57
Chapter Five	72
Chapter Six	81
Chapter Seven	97
Chapter Eight	110
Chapter Nine	126
Chapter Ten	136
Chapter Eleven	158
Chapter Twelve	171
Chapter Thirteen	184

Chapter 1

Woodsborough, New Jersey
1942

Annie twisted in her sleep. In her dream she was running, running, trying with all her might to scream, "No, Mama, No!" but could not utter a sound.

She jerked awake. A shuddering gasp shook her. Her heart pounded in her chest. Every cell in her body was tensed with terror. For a long time, she lay rigidly still on her back, scarcely breathing, staring at the slanted ceiling above her. Sobs struggled in her, but could not come through.

Finally, barely daring to move, she turned her head. Early morning light poured through the window. Outside she could see the leaves and branches of the tree that grew close by. She became aware of the sound of Donny snoring. Turning her head the other way, she saw him in his narrow bed next to hers. He was asleep with his mouth slightly open, clutching his ragged teddy bear, his tumbled curls dark against his white pillow.

Annie caught a swift, short breath. It was a dream. She was in her and Donny's room and it was morning.

There was a soft thud on the windowsill. Her cat Misty was poised there, the morning light shining on her gray fur. She leaped lightly down. Then Annie felt the familiar, comforting weight of the cat on her bed, the pressure of soft paws walking up her body. Misty licked Annie's face with her rough pink tongue, then settled down on her chest.

A long sigh rippled through Annie's body, loosening the fibers of her fear. She rolled on her side and gathered her cat close in her arms. "Oh, Misty," she whispered. "I had a really bad dream."

Misty's purr vibrated into Annie's aching heart. She bent her face into the soft gray fur and began to cry.

Her bed shifted. Annie turned her head and looked up to see Donny leaning over her. She could smell the warm flannelly odor of his sweat.

"Hey, Annie-fanny. What's wrong?"

Annie sucked up a sob. "I had a bad dream."

"What did you dream this time?"

"Goblins were chasing me … through the big woods. They were all pale with big bulgy eyes and long arms like worms and were trying to grab me … to take me to the witch. I was running as fast as I could, but they …" Annie's words were interrupted by sobs. "I fell down, and they almost got me… Then Mama came and I was running to her to be safe … but she got all big and dark, and her nose got long, and … and she was smiling a mean smile with pointy yellow teeth … and when she held out her arms, she had claws instead of hands … and she was reaching out to grab me … *Mama* was the witch."

Shaken with a fresh burst of sobs, Annie turned away from Donny and bent her head over Misty again.

"Aw. Don't cry." Donny patted her head. "Mama's not a witch. She's mean sometimes, but lots of times she's nice. I know a secret. Will you promise not to tell?"

Still curled over her cat, Annie nodded. She stopped sobbing to listen.

"Remember tomorrow's your birthday. You're gonna be five. Mama's gonna make you a cake. She told me. And she has a present for you."

After breakfast Donny rode off on his bike to play with his friend, Jack. Annie sat on the front steps of their house, watching him go.

Annie didn't have any friends. The only girl around who was Annie's age lived more than a mile up the road. Bossy Linda. Sometimes Mama would take her up to visit, but it was a long walk, and Annie didn't like Linda very much.

Annie kicked her feet against the stone steps. She was hungry. They'd had toast and yellow juice for breakfast, but Mama had burned the toast. She always did. By the time she'd scraped the burned part off into the sink, the toast was thin. Even with peanut butter on it, it didn't begin to fill Annie up.

She wished they still lived with Grandma and Aunt Nellie. There was always plenty to eat there. Grandma had a big house with lots of rooms. She and Donny had each had their own room and there was a staircase with a banister that she and Donny could slide down. And Aunt Nellie was nice. She held Annie in her lap and let her follow her around and help make cookies.

Mama didn't like it there, so they moved. But Mama didn't like this house either.

It was a little house made out of stone, like some of the houses in her fairytale book. It was way away from other houses, sitting on the side of a hill. Below the house, the road went by, and behind the house were big woods.

Every house was better when Daddy was home, but now Daddy was far away in Boston looking for a job.

Annie loved her Daddy more than anyone in the world, and the ache of missing him was always with her. When he was home, he laughed and sang and played the piano, carried her in his arms and tossed her in the air until she screamed with joy. Sometimes when he was away he sent her a letter telling her the adventures of her teddy bear, who, he claimed, came to visit him in Boston and got into all kinds of trouble. Mama would smile and even laugh with Annie when she read the letters to her. Annie knew Mama missed him, too. Donny said that was why she was so crabby.

Mama came out the front door and sat on the steps beside Annie. Annie leaned against her. The dream had faded away. It felt good to have Mama near her.

"What are you going to do today?" Mama asked.

"I don't know. Maybe I'll go up in the woods."

"All by yourself? Donny's gone off to play with Jack."

"I know. I could go all by myself. I'm almost five."

"That's true. You're getting to be such a big girl. But those are big woods. What would you do?"

"I could play in the fort me and Donny made."

"Donny and I."

"Donny and I. I like to look at things, bugs and flowers. Sometimes there's squirrels."

"That sounds nice. I wish I could go with you."

Mama couldn't go up in the woods because there was so much poison ivy and she got sick from it. Annie and Donny and Daddy sometimes got a little rash, but nothing bad like what happened to Mama. Annie knew how to stay away from poison ivy. Her daddy had shown her and Donny the three shiny leaves. All the same, Mama made them wear long pants and shoes whenever they played up there, no matter how hot it was.

Mama frowned and rubbed her forehead. "I guess it's all right for you to go by yourself. But don't go far. Put on your overalls, and watch out for poison ivy. And come home right away when I ring the bell."

"Okay."

Mama got up, brushed her hand over Annie's hair, and went inside.

Annie sat a while longer on the steps. She thought about her birthday, and Donny telling her Mama would have a cake and a present for her. Last year, her present had been Misty, who'd been a tiny gray kitten then, the best present she'd ever had. She wondered what it would be this year. How could Mama give her a cake and a present when they didn't even have enough money for food? But maybe present money was different from food money.

She was excited about her birthday. She would be five, and when school started she would go to kindergarten. Donny would be in third grade and he would ride her to school on the bar on the front of his bike, though Mama had promised to walk with her the first day. In kindergarten, Mama said, there would be lots of little girls who would become her friends.

Maybe.

Annie got up from the step and went upstairs. Misty lay on Annie's bed, curled up on her pillow.

"I'm going to the woods," Annie told her. "You want to come with me?"

Misty had often gone with her and Donny, scampering along after them, playing with leaves and stalking bugs while they worked on their fort, but she hadn't come recently. Misty stretched and yawned showing her small white teeth and pink tongue, then curled up again. Annie could see how her tummy bulged when she stretched. Mama had told Annie that Misty's tummy was big because she had babies inside that would be born soon. Sometimes when Annie put her hand on Misty's belly she could feel the babies moving inside. It felt to her like magic, like a fairy tale, that baby kittens could be inside her big kitten. She couldn't wait for them to be born.

"When will they come out?" she'd asked her mama a few days ago.

"I don't know," Mama had said.

Annie couldn't believe that. Mama always knew the answer to everything. Maybe she just didn't want to tell.

"Will the babies look like Misty, like people say I look like you?"

"I don't know that either," her mama had said, smiling. She was in a gentle mood that day, holding Annie on her lap and stroking her hair. "Maybe some of them will look like their daddy."

The babies had a daddy?

"Who is their daddy?"

"I think he's the big yellow tomcat that lives in the house up the road."

"Will he come live with us when the babies are born, to take care of them?"

"No. Cats don't do that. Only people. Daddy cats start their babies and then just go away."

"Don't they come back?"

"Not usually."

"Our daddy is people. Is he going to come back?"

Then Mama's voice had gone from gentle to sharp. "That's enough questions." She dumped Annie off her lap and walked away fast.

Annie sat on the bed, pushing her lower lip out, aching inside as she remembered how Mama had pushed her away. Mama's gentle moods could end so fast if Annie said or did the wrong thing. And she never meant to do anything wrong. She just didn't know what all the wrong things were.

She put her hand on Misty's soft fur. Misty purred and looked up at Annie with her big green eyes, and Annie was comforted. She kissed Misty on the top of her head, and went to look for her overalls, feeling a shiver of excitement about going up into the woods all by herself.

She counted the stairs as she went down. She was proud that she could count to one hundred. Her daddy had taught her, and now her mama was teaching her to read. She reached the bottom of the steps. She wanted to jump off the last one and shout the number, but maybe Mama had a headache.

"Twelve," she whispered as she stepped softly off the bottom step.

She peeked into the living room. Mama was sitting in the big chair, reading. She got mad if anyone disturbed her when she was reading. Annie crept by quietly, through the dining room and kitchen and out the back door.

Outside the door were the big rain barrel, the trash can, the gray washtubs, and a shed where Daddy stored his tools and Donny parked his bike. There was only a little yard. The woods came down almost to the house.

　　　　　　　　　　☙ ❧

Meg lifted her head from the *Ladies' Home Journal* just in time to catch a glimpse of Annie slipping by the living room door. So quietly, like a little shadow. She was always so quiet Meg never knew where she was.

She was probably on her way up the hill. Meg hoped she had her overalls on. She'd better check and be sure.

She laid down her magazine with a sigh. She shouldn't be reading foolish stories in a magazine anyway. Pure escape, that's what it was. She hadn't washed the dishes and the kitchen floor was sticky from the children spilling juice on it.

She got up and reached the kitchen window just in time to see Annie starting up the path into the woods.

She's so little, Meg thought with a pang. Way too thin. If only I could give her a decent meal. She'd been hoarding a can of tuna fish. Maybe she'd get it out for Annie's lunch. Donny was invited to Jack's. He'd get a good meal there. And with him gone, there would be more for Annie. She could give Annie some carrot sticks with it.

She watched until Annie disappeared into the trees. She did have her overalls on. She was a good little girl.

Meg sighed again and rubbed her neck. The dull ache in the back of her head was starting already, so early in the day. Time to get to work anyway. She turned on the tap. No hot water. Damn! She'd forgotten to turn on the boiler after breakfast. She found the matches and knelt down to light it.

She was tempted to go back to reading her magazine story while the water heated, but she shouldn't be reading that junk anyway. Instead, she just sat down on the floor, hunched over by the boiler, her head in her hand.

Her thoughts circled around in the same familiar, despairing loop.

She hadn't guessed it would be so hard. They should have stayed at the farm with Mama and Nellie. At least there the children had enough to eat.

But those two were so good and proper and Christian-kind. They tried to be nice to her, but she could tell how shocked they were by her bad temper. She could imagine them wondering how their Jesse could have married someone like her. She had felt so judged. She couldn't stand it. And Annie was bonding with Nellie more and more, clearly loving her better than her own mother.

So now she was alone in this damnable house, so small they could barely fit in the necessary furniture.

Meg shifted her weight. The stone floor was hard. The pathetic kitchen was so tiny there wasn't even room for a chair. She got up and went into the dining room. It was only big enough for the table and four chairs, one of which was always empty. She pulled out a chair, dropped into it, and laid her arms and head on the table.

She was so tired. So tired of all the drudgery. She hated the house and the humid August heat. Her body twitched. She got up again, kicked her chair back, and pushed her limp hair off her brow. She had to use the bathroom.

She strode into the little square hall at the bottom of the stairs. The front door opened into it with a view straight up the stairs and into the bathroom. Who would design a house that way? It was embarrassing. Not that anyone came to visit them.

Upstairs it was already stuffy and hot. Only three windows up there—one in the bathroom and one in each bedroom.

Chapter One

The water was warm when she washed her hands after using the toilet. Maybe warm enough to wash the dishes and mop the floor. Just what she was longing to do. She turned off the faucet with a jerk.

At the bottom of the stairs, she stopped and looked into the living room. Her internal rant about the inadequacies of the house crescendoed. There was barely space to walk across the living room, crammed as it was with only one bookcase, one comfortable chair, the couch, Victrola, the piano. But Jesse couldn't be without music. Nor could she. The piano needed tuning, but that cost money. Probably there wasn't a piano tuner to be found for miles around anyway.

This miserable house was a far cry from the spacious home overlooking the Pacific Ocean where she'd grown up. Her mother hadn't had to prepare meals or wash dishes. She certainly didn't have to shovel coal into the furnace, or mow the lawn. In the elegant home where Meg had grown up there were servants for all that. There was even a nanny to take care of the children until they started school.

That house was long gone now. Passed on to her brother after their parents died and then sold. She'd inherited furniture, linens, china, but there was no room for them here. Too big and elegant for this crummy house, they were all stored in a spare bedroom at Mama's and Nellie's.

She really needed to mow the lawn. She looked out at it through the open front door. Only a small part next to the house was level. The rest sloped down steeply to the road. It was a struggle to push the mower up and down the steep part, and the lawn was all weeds and stubble anyway.

The ache in the back of her head had morphed into pounding in her temples. She turned away from the door and walked back to the kitchen.

Just get the dishes washed. She put the plug in the sink, turned on the faucet, picked up the soap cage and swished it through the water. It was barely hot enough to make suds, but Meg didn't care. There weren't many dishes because there wasn't much food. Just a plate and a glass for herself and each of the children. Her coffee mug with an inch of cold coffee in the bottom. She drank the dregs, and put all the dishes into the soapy water.

Then she just stood there, hands in the water, thinking of her children. Donny going to school with factory workers' children who didn't speak decent English, and Annie soon to start kindergarten. She should keep Annie home, not expose her to those rough children and ignorant teachers. Donny managed okay. He had a strong spirit. But Annie ...

Jesse gone.

But there was nothing for him here. Working on a road crew, digging ditches. He with his refinement, his intellect, his Ph.D. He said it was a good experience for a sociologist. Always making the best of things.

She missed him so much. His gentle touch, his loving smile, his quick humor and the way he teased her and made her laugh, his clear tenor singing in the shower, the evenings when he sat at the piano and filled the house with music. She'd never known a man like him who paid so much attention to his children and even helped with the housework when he was home.

Meg realized she was squeezing the dishcloth into a knot and that her tears were dripping into the water. She pulled in a ragged breath and wiped her cheeks with the back of her wet hand. Much good that did. Just get the damned dishes washed.

Her hands moved, rinsing, stacking. If only Jesse could come home more often. But there was gas rationing, and anyway gas cost money, as did long distance phone calls. At least he was too old to be in the war.

He had called two nights ago. Told her to have hope. He had an interview coming up at Boston University. He was staying with his older brother, a professor at some small college in Boston, Meg couldn't remember which. His brother had gotten him some tutoring jobs. He could send some money soon.

Chapter One

Annie followed a path she and Donny had made. It led a short way up through the trees to a flat-topped cliff that jutted out of the hillside. Above it three huge trees hung their branches down so low that it was like a roof over the cliff. Donny had decided that it was a perfect place for a fort. They had worked on it for weeks, digging rocks out of the ground with a trowel and piling them along the front edge of the cliff to make a wall. Annie didn't especially enjoy fort building, but Donny had it all planned and Annie had to do what he said.

Today Donny wasn't there. Annie could do what she wanted.

She sat a while in the fort. It was quiet without Donny talking all the time and telling her what to do. She could hear some birds chirping a little way up the hill, and even the sound of a soft breeze moving through the leaves of the trees above her.

After a while she crawled through the opening they had left for a door and looked up the hill. The woods looked mysterious, magical, like the pictures in Annie's fairytale book. Annie loved the delicate ferns around her feet, the smell of the dark earth, the way the bushes pushed close with vines winding in them, the tall tree trunks rising up. She especially loved the way the sun came through the leaves, making leaf shadows dance all around her when the breeze moved.

She and Donny had been so busy with the fort, they had never explored much. A little above the fort, she saw a faint track through the undergrowth, a path she hadn't noticed before. It wound up and away into the trees. Who had made the path? She knew there were no other children nearby. It must have been made by an animal.

Mama said not to go far. She'd just go a little way.

The path was open about as high as her shoulders; above that branches and vines hung over and she had to duck her head to get through. It must have been a big animal, to clear the path so high. Maybe if she was very quiet, she might see it.

She knew how to be quiet so as not to disturb her mother when she had a headache. She had to watch where she put her foot so nothing would squeak, like the third board outside her and Donny's room; she had to open and close the screen door very carefully so there were no creaks or bangs. Now she had to be careful not to rustle leaves as she pushed the branches aside, or kick a stone, or step on a twig that might snap. She went slowly up the path, practicing quietness.

A sudden jabber overhead startled her. She looked up to see a squirrel on the branch above her. It continued to jabber, flicking its tail in swift ripples that showed its bright orange underside.

Annie laughed. "You don't have to be so mad," she told it. "I'm not going to hurt you. See, I'm leaving."

A little farther on, a rotting log lay across her path. Ferns grew out of it, sheltering a wide crack at one end. Annie peered into the crack. It was a big log and the crack was so deep she couldn't see the bottom of it. Maybe it was a doorway to the elves' kingdom. A thrill of excitement ran through her. She lifted her head and looked around. The woods felt even more magical than when she had first entered. Maybe this *was* a magic woods. Maybe there really were elves. She knew Donny would say they were just pretend, but Donny didn't know everything. She wondered what Daddy would say.

When she stood up, a soft breeze moved through the woods, and a tree branch hanging over her brushed her hair with its leaves. Her heart opened and she looked up into the branches above. Dappled sunlight fell across her face and it seemed the tree whispered a secret to her. In a magic woods trees could whisper to you.

She looked down again into the crack in the log. Maybe if she sat there quietly, elves would come out. But she was also lured by the faint animal path she had been following.

The path won. She ducked under a big branch and pushed through a tangle of bushes and vines. Whatever animal made the path must have jumped over that part, but she could see the path opening again on the other side, leading to a little grassy clearing.

Annie took a few steps forward, then went perfectly still, her eyes wide. Three deer grazed in the little clearing. One of them was bigger, the other two smaller. Maybe it was a mama and her babies. The mama deer lifted her head and perked up her big, pointed ears. Her soft, dark eyes looked straight at Annie. Annie held still, so still, barely breathing. For a long moment, she and the mama deer gazed at each other.

The mama deer moved her ears, turning them slightly from side to side. Then she flicked her tail, turned, and leaped lightly over some low bushes at the edge of the clearing. The two young ones followed. In a flash, all three had disappeared into the trees.

Annie let out her breath. "Oh …," she whispered.

It was the deer who had made the path, Annie was sure, jumping over the thick places just as she had guessed. She still held the image of them leaping, arcing over the bushes, so lightly, so easily. If only she could leap like that.

Annie stepped into the little clearing and lay down in the grass. It was kind of tickley on her bare arms and neck, but still it felt good to lie in it. The trees around the clearing towered over her, their leaves in different shades of green and their dark branches vivid against the blue sky. A soft wind moved through them, turning the leaves.

Peace flowed through Annie. She sighed a long sigh, feeling her body soften into the earth.

As she lay quietly looking up into the trees, it seemed in one moment as if the sky, so blue, was right behind the leaves, right up against them. In the next moment the sky was far away, so deep a leaf could never touch it. She lay a long time, first seeing it one way, then the other. Could they both be true? She'd have to ask Mama. But maybe Mama wouldn't be interested.

Daddy would for sure. If only she could ask Daddy. But maybe Daddy wouldn't come back. Maybe he was like the daddy cat that just started his babies and then left. Maybe that's why Mama pushed Annie off her lap, because she was sad about it.

The ache of missing her daddy tightened her chest. With a swift roll, she jumped up, her peace shattered. She pushed around the bush the deer had leaped over and ran up the path that opened on the other side. She wasn't trying to be quiet anymore. She was just running as fast as she could away from the fear her Daddy might never come back.

❦

Meg flipped the *Ladies' Home Journal* shut and tossed it down on the little table beside her chair. After she'd washed the dishes and mopped the kitchen floor, she had surrendered to her curiosity about how the story ended. It was a stupid story, blah, cliché. Maybe she should take up writing stories for magazines. She could certainly do better than that.

Oh, no! She'd forgotten to turn off the boiler. Their landlord had warned them that if they left it on too long, the pressure would build up and it might explode. Comforting thought.

She went to the kitchen and turned off the boiler. The kitchen window looked out into the woods. Even though she'd told Annie that she wished she could go with her, she had no desire to enter the woods. She didn't like them. They loomed over the house and were thick with bushes, tangled with vines. Especially poison ivy vines. Her one venture into the woods, when Jesse had coaxed her to explore with him and the children, had resulted in weeks of utter misery. She wished the children weren't so attracted to playing up there. Fortunately they weren't as allergic to poison ivy as she was. Still …

Annie should be back soon. Meg had told her not to be gone long. She checked her watch. Ten thirty. When had Annie left? Somewhere around nine. An hour and a half. What would she do up there all by herself? It was time for her to come home now. Meg was uneasy about her going alone. Maybe she shouldn't have given her permission.

She picked up the big bell she used to call the children, stepped out the back door and rang it.

☙ ❧

The woods became more open. Annie could no longer see the deer path, but she kept on running up the hillside. She came to a place where a steep rock face blocked her way. Above and around it, the trees closed in again. The cliff was high, as high as her bedroom window. She leaned against it, panting from her run.

She looked up at the cliff. It would be fun to be on top. Donny would climb up there for sure. She could do it. Beside the cliff, the bank was steep under the trees, but she went up easily on her hands and feet, pushing the vines and bushes aside, creating a tunnel in the undergrowth. At the top, there was a broad rocky shelf as big as her bedroom, spreading back to where the trees started again, rising on up the hill.

From the top of the cliff she could see everything. Her house far below, just the roof half hidden by the trees. Below that, the road, like a long curvy black snake, wound out of sight around a bend in one direction, and led into town on the other. In the town, she could see the cluster of houses, the three churches with their steeples, the school with the playground around it, and the factory with black smoke puffing out of its chimneys.

She felt like a bird, being up there so high, looking down on the world below. A gust of wind rose up from the valley, blowing her curls back from her face, rippling through her T-shirt and cooling the sweat on her chest. She lifted her arms and turned her face up to the sky, sudden joy pulsing through her.

But the sun was hot. One of the trees just above the cliff and off to the side where she had climbed up, was an old, tall spruce. It towered against the sky, and its dark branches touched the ground all around it.

It would be shady under the tree. Annie went to it, pushed aside one branch and looked underneath. It was a perfect shelter, almost a circle around the big, rough trunk in the center. Annie crawled in. It was dim inside, and definitely cooler out of the sun. The ground was covered in dried spruce needles, soft and deep. Annie scooped some up in her hands, inhaling their pungent fragrance. They were small and prickly, but there were many layers and the surface was smooth, as if no one had come there to disturb it before Annie.

She looked around more carefully. The space under the tree wasn't a circle after all. On the far side of the trunk, another cliff face, about as tall as Annie, interrupted the curve. And oh! There was a dark space in the rock, a hole, a cave! Annie scrambled toward it, first crawling, then finding as she neared the trunk that she could stand. Beyond the trunk, the cliff held the branches up so she could stand there, too.

She had to get down on her hands and knees to look into the hole. It was big. Big enough for her to crawl into, and once inside, high enough for her to sit. She crawled to the very back of the cave. She tried lying down. The cave was long enough if she curled up.

Annie sat up in the middle of the cave and looked out into the dim space under the tree. She was brimming with excitement. This was a perfect hidey hole, way better than Donny's old fort. She lay down again, curled on her side, looking out into the dim light under the tree, feeling doubly sheltered by tree and cave.

But the floor of the cave was rough and rocky. Pointy rocks were poking into her. She got up on her hands and knees and started at the back of the cave raking the loose stones with her fingers, backing out as she pulled them to the opening of the cave. But some of the pointy rocks were part of the floor. As she backed out of the cave and her knees touched the cushion of spruce needles, she had an idea.

She piled the loose rocks by the opening of the cave, then began gathering big handfuls of spruce needles. She crawled back into the cave and spread them over the hard, rocky floor. It took a lot of spruce needles to cover the whole floor thickly enough that the pointy rocks wouldn't poke through, but there were lots. She gathered the needles from all around the tree and filled in the hollows where she had taken them, so the space under the tree would still be smooth and even.

At last she finished. The floor of the cave was soft and comfy. She lay down, curled on her side, her head resting on her arm.

⊱ ⊰

Meg sat at the dining room table where she had been pondering their bills, trying to figure out how little she could pay each one and still keep the gas and electric and phone turned on, how to eke out the last of the money from the road crew job. She glanced at her watch. Eleven o'clock. Annie still hadn't come back. Meg had told her not to go too far. She should have come right away when Meg rang the bell.

She stood up and went to the kitchen window. Why wasn't Annie back? Meg had lost track of time dealing with the damn bills. It had been a half hour since she rang the bell. Annie had always been an obedient child. She must not have heard the bell.

Prickles of panic rose up Meg's spine. Where could Annie be? Why wouldn't she have heard the bell? Anything could happen. She could fall. Donny had said there were cliffs up there.

Meg hurried into the kitchen, grabbed the bell, went out and rang it again, longer, louder.

"Annie," she called as loudly as she could. "Annie, come home."

She stared up the path that led from the back yard. The woods stared back at her, secret and still.

For the next hour, again and again, Meg went out the back door, rang and called.

She crossed the small yard and stood at the opening in the trees. Just to the side of the path the children had made, she saw the vine with the three shiny leaves. She stepped back.

If only she weren't so allergic, she'd go look for Annie. But she remembered all too vividly the raging fever, the oozing blisters that lasted for weeks. If she got sick like that again, who would take care of the children?

The noon whistle sounded. Annie had been gone for three hours. Maybe she was lost. Meg didn't know how far the woods went, up and over the hill.

She clutched her throat. Maybe she should call Jack's mother, have her send Donny home to search for Annie. But what if he got lost, too?

Hammers pounded on the inside of her head. Her belly churned with nausea. She went to the kitchen sink, wet a towel in cold water and pressed it to her eyes and brow. Again she went out, rang and called, "Annie, Annie."

Annie was waked by the factory whistle. It sounded at regular times through the day and night. Mama had told her that it was to tell the workers that they could change shifts. Annie didn't understand what that meant, but she knew one of the whistles sounded at lunch time.

Lunch time! Mama had said not to stay long, and she had been gone all morning. She hadn't heard Mama ring the bell, but she realized she was so far up the hill, that maybe she couldn't hear it. It wasn't near as loud as the factory whistle.

Oh! Mama would be really mad. Annie felt scared in her tummy. She crawled out of her cave and stood up by the trunk of the tree. Even though her tummy was still queasy, she was happy. This was her tree, her cave. She'd found it all by herself and fixed it up. She could come back again, and no one would know where she was.

But she'd better get going. She dropped to her hands and knees and crawled out from under her tree. Still on her hands and knees, she backed into her tunnel down the steep bank beside the cliff. She came to her feet at the bottom and looked down over the area below where the trees grew thinner. Farther down the forest became thick again, and she couldn't see the path she had taken. What if she couldn't find her way home?

She'd have to try. She remembered that when she had walked in the woods with her daddy the last time he was home, he'd said she could always find her way home by just going downhill. So she started down. When she reached the thicker forest, she did find her path, branches she had pushed aside that hadn't gone back to their place, a faint opening in the underbrush. She followed it. She came to the little glade where she had seen the deer, a bit farther on, the log that might be an elf home, the tree where the squirrel had jabbered at her. It wasn't there now; the woods were quiet.

She began to hurry a little. There was the fort, and the path clear now toward home. She walked the path from fort to home more slowly. Maybe Mama wouldn't be mad, but ... fragments of her dream brushed behind her eyes.

When she reached the edge of the woods and could look down into her backyard, she hid behind a thicket. She could see the kitchen window. Her mama was there, probably working at the sink. She wasn't looking out. Maybe Annie could sneak around and go in the front door and upstairs and hide in her room, pretend she'd been there for a long time.

Her heart was beating fast now. She backed up into the woods and crept around toward the side of the house where the living room was. She'd still have to make a dash across the back yard. She was hesitating, trembling, when Mama came out the back door and looked up the hill. She had the bell in her hand. She rang it and called, "Annie, Annie, where are you? Come home, *now!*"

She sounded sad and afraid.

Mama afraid? Annie's heart opened. Maybe Mama loved her and was worried she was lost.

She burst out of the shelter of trees and ran to her mama. "I'm here. Here I am, Mama."

Mama dropped the bell and picked Annie up, holding her tight in her arms. Just for a moment. Then she set Annie down. She towered over her. She grabbed Annie by the shoulders and started shaking her.

"Where have you been? I told you to come home when I rang the bell. I have rung and rung for hours and you didn't come. Wicked, wicked girl. I give you freedom and you abuse it. You're not ever going up in the woods again alone."

She was shaking Annie so hard that her head was bobbing all around. Her hands were gripping Annie's shoulders like the witch's claws in her dream.

But worst of all was her saying Annie couldn't go into the woods alone anymore.

Mama was still yelling at her, but now Annie was crying so hard she couldn't hear what Mama was saying.

Mama let go of her shoulders and slapped her hard across her face.

Annie ran. Through the kitchen, the dining room, up the stairs, into the bedroom, and under the bed.

Meg chased Annie as far as the dining room. There she stopped. She heard Annie running up the stairs, heard her sobs, the slam of the bedroom door. Meg dropped into a chair and covered her face with her hands, sick with grief and self-loathing. Why, why had she shaken and slapped her child? Again. Oh, my Annie, she mourned. I hit her so hard her head went way over to one side. I could have broken her neck. She is so little, so fragile. She came running to me with her beautiful smile. I was holding her precious little body safe in my arms at last, and then ... fierce, cruel demon inside of me. How could I have hit her so hard?

She lifted her head and listened. No sound from upstairs. When Annie went into silence, it was much harder to reach her than when she was still crying. She would go far away. Sometimes only Jesse could reach her. And Jesse was gone.

Meg got up from her chair. She'd have to try. The longer the silence, the worse it got.

She climbed the stairs, opened the bedroom door, knelt down by Annie's bed, and moved the bedspread aside. It was as she feared. Annie was curled into a tight ball way up under the head of the bed.

"Annie," Meg said softly, "I'm sorry I hit you. I was just so worried when you were gone so long. Please come out."

Annie didn't move or answer.

Meg stifled an impulse to crawl under the bed and drag her out. She'd done that before, but it only made matters worse.

"Annie, come out now."

Still no response.

Meg leaned her head against the side of the bed and began to cry.

※

Annie lay listening to her mama's sobs. Mamas shouldn't cry. They were big and could do anything they wanted. Still, she knew Mama cried sometimes. Then Daddy would comfort her. She'd lie on the couch with her head in his lap and he would smooth her hair and she'd stop crying.

But Daddy was gone.

Annie knew she was bad. Her mama's words "wicked, wicked girl" burned in her heart. She had worried Mama so much it made her cry. Being up in the magic woods and finding the cave was the best fun Annie had ever had, and now it was all spoiled. Mama would never let her go again. Annie wanted to cry, too, but she was all stopped up. Her tummy hurt.

She curled her legs up tighter and went away—away from Mama's crying, away from being bad. She was standing on the cliff again with the wind blowing through her shirt. She was sitting in her cave, safe. She was strong. She would be five tomorrow and she'd found a hidey hole way better than Donny's fort. It was her castle. She was a princess and Misty was her magic cat. Elves would come and be her friends and bring her magic food. At night she and Misty would go with them into the forest and dance under the moon with all the animals, the squirrel with the ripply tail and the mama deer and her babies.

The bed shifted. Mama wasn't leaning on it anymore. She had stopped crying and was lifting the corner of the bedspread. Annie could feel the change in the light through her closed eyes. She wasn't in her castle. She was under her bed. Her cheek still burned where Mama had slapped her. She was bad and really sad.

Her mama said, "Annie, please come out. It's lunch time. I know you must be hungry. I have tuna fish and carrot sticks for your lunch. Please come out and let me hold you and comfort you."

It was Mama's gentle voice. Everything in Annie ached to be held. And she was so hungry. Tuna fish. But Mama's gentle could change so fast. She didn't want Mama to yell at her and hit her again.

A darkness of confusion overcame her—fear and longing battering her back and forth. Longing was stronger. Slowly her legs uncurled. With a shuddering sigh, she turned herself around and crawled toward the light where the bedspread was lifted.

Chapter 2

Annie lay in bed curled on her side, her eyes open, looking out the window at the tree outside and the early morning sunlight shining through its leaves. She saw the sky right up against the tree and at the same time far, far away, as she had the day before, lying in the little meadow where she had seen the deer.

She was happy inside. The day before, after she'd come out from under the bed, Mama had been gentle all the rest of the day. She'd held Annie a long time and kissed her and given her tuna fish for lunch, and Annie's tummy had been full for the first time in a long time.

Annie lay looking at the tree and the sky a while longer, cherishing her happiness. She had told Mama about the tree and the sky, and Mama *was* interested. She said it was both true, that sky was all around the tree and also far away.

Then Annie remembered that today was her birthday. She was five and would go to school soon. She was a big girl. She could be responsible now, the way Mama was always telling Donny to be. Maybe if she were really, really good, and never did anything that would make Mama worried or mad, Mama would stay gentle. Annie loved her when she was gentle, and it seemed then that Mama loved her, too. Maybe she really did.

Annie turned over. Donny was gone. He'd gotten up so quietly she didn't even hear him. Where was Misty? She must have gone out the window through the corner where the screen was loose and down the tree to pee like she did sometimes in the morning.

Annie let out a long sigh and stretched out on her back. Her feet touched something wet. Oh, no! Had she wet her bed? But her pajamas weren't wet. The wet was at the bottom of the bed.

She sat up and turned the sheet back. Her eyes widened. There was Misty, curled on her side, and leaning up against her tummy were tiny little creatures, some yellow and some gray. Misty looked up at Annie and gave a small, chirping meow as if to say, "Look what I've done." She seemed to be smiling.

The little tiny creatures must be her babies!

"Misty," Annie whispered. "Did your babies come out? Are these your babies?"

As if in answer, Misty began purring and bent her head to lick one of yellow ones.

Barely breathing, Annie bent down and counted the babies. There were five. Two were yellow, two gray, and one a mixture of gray and yellow. Misty had given her five kittens for her birthday!

The babies looked wet. Maybe Misty had been licking them all. Then Annie noticed the sheet underneath them was wet, and there were red blotches on it. Was it blood? Was Misty hurt?

She had to ask Mama.

Carefully, she laid the sheet back over Misty and her babies. Then she dashed out of the bedroom and down the stairs, calling, "Mama, Mama, Misty's babies came out in the bottom of my bed!"

Mama came to meet her, picked her up and hugged her. "Happy birthday, Annie. Misty's babies are born? Where are they?"

"They're in my bed, down at the bottom. But, Mama, the sheet is all wet under them and there's red on the sheet, like blood. Is Misty hurt?"

"I don't think so. Let's go see."

Mama took her hand and they went up the stairs together. Annie went to her bed and turned down the sheet, and Mama came and looked at Misty and her babies.

"Oh, my," she said. "Five of them."

"For my five birthday." Annie jumped with excitement. "Misty gave me five kittens for my five birthday."

"Looks like she did. And that yellow cat up the road is the daddy, as I guessed."

"But, Mama, is that blood on the sheet? Is Misty hurt?"

"It's okay, honey. There is usually blood when babies are born. Don't worry. Misty looks fine. But we need to clean up your bed. Let's get a basket for Misty and her kittens and put a soft towel in it, so she'll have a dry, cozy place to take care of them. Then we'll put a clean sheet on your bed. You know, Misty having her babies in your bed means she really trusts you. Lots of mother cats hide away when their babies are born."

Annie felt a surge of happiness that Misty trusted her. But she knew Misty did. She and Misty were best friends.

Donny came upstairs. "I wanna see Misty's kittens." He came over and looked at the kittens on the bed. "They look like little rats."

"They do not!" Annie protested.

Donny shrugged. "They'll look better later. Ned's cat had kittens last spring, and they looked like that at first, but then their eyes opened and their ears perked up and they were pretty cute. Ma, can I go to Jack's today?"

"Yes, after breakfast. But I want you to come home in the afternoon, so we can celebrate Annie's birthday."

"Okay, sure." Donny went back downstairs. Annie didn't think he was very interested in her kittens. She looked down again at Misty's babies.

"Mama, they're so tiny."

"They'll grow fast. See, Misty is a good mother. She's nursing them, giving them milk from her nipples so that they can get big and strong."

"Oh!" Annie looked closer and saw that the babies were sucking on Misty's nipples. How could Misty make milk inside her? "Can I cuddle the babies?" she asked Mama.

"Not yet. They're still so new they just need to be with their mother. You could touch them with the tip of your finger, but very gently, just a little."

Annie leaned over and touched each kitten, very softly with the tip of her finger, her heart bursting with tenderness and joy.

"Can I still pet Misty?"

"Of course."

Annie stroked Misty's head. Misty purred and looked up at Annie with her wide green eyes.

"Come," Mama said, taking Annie's hand. "Let's go find a basket. I think I have one down in the kitchen that will be just right."

Meg led Annie down the stairs and into the kitchen. Annie's trusting little hand in hers. Annie looking up at her, shining with happiness. How sweet and beautiful she was when she was happy. Meg held her hand a little tighter, vowing inwardly not to crush that happiness as she had too often, too recently.

Meg had a collection of baskets she was fond of, stored on a high shelf in the pantry. She hadn't been able to bear leaving them at Mama's and Nellie's with all her other nice things.

She had one basket in mind for the kittens, not one of her very best ones. She pulled a stool over, stood on it, and brought the baskets down. The one she planned for the kittens was one of the plainer ones, dark brown on the sides with beige wicker around the top and bottom. She lifted it out and showed it to Annie.

But Annie was looking at a slightly bigger one, cream and pale green woven together with pink rosettes scattered around the sides, and an arched handle. It was Meg's favorite.

"This one is so pretty," Annie said. "Let's use this one."

"Well, that's kind of a special basket."

"Then that's perfect, 'cause Misty's kittens are special."

Meg cringed inwardly. She really didn't want a bunch of kittens scrabbling around in her favorite basket, excreting in it. But Annie looked so pleased with it. Maybe she could trade it out in a day or two. "Okay, we'll use this one."

"Goody! Let's put a pink towel in it, to match the pink flowers."

Annie ran her fingers over the side of the basket. Meg could see her appreciating the texture and the colors. But a pink towel. No! The pink towels were the best and newest and Meg had so few of her nice things left. She'd planned to line the basket with some old raggedy towels. A brief battle erupted inside her. Not one of her best towels. But it was Annie's birthday.

"All right," she said. "Just for today. We'll need to change the towels each day to keep the basket clean."

"I'll get the pink towel. I know right where it is. Pink is Misty's favorite color."

Annie ran ahead of her up the stairs to the linen closet in the bathroom. Meg followed more slowly, carrying her favorite basket.

In the bedroom, Annie arranged the pink towel in the basket. It did look very nice. Meg put the basket beside the bed and turned down the sheet.

"Now we need to pick the kittens up very carefully and put them into the basket. I'd better do it."

"No, Mama, let me do it. I can be very careful."

"All right. But let me move the first one and show you how. See, you want to slide your hand under the whole body so the legs don't dangle."

Meg slid her hand under the gray and yellow kitten and lifted it up. It let out a piercing squeal.

"Oh, don't hurt it!" Annie cried.

"I'm not hurting it. It's just scared to be away from its mother."

Misty stood on the bed watching intently as Meg lowered the squealing kitten into the basket. The minute Meg took her hand away, Misty jumped in and began licking it. The squealing stopped.

"Let me now." Annie went up to the bed.

"Don't squeeze it," Meg said.

"Mama, I wouldn't squeeze it."

Annie stroked one of the gray kittens with her fingertip. "Don't be scared," she said to it, her voice soft and loving. "I'm just going to move you into the basket so you can be with your sister and mother." Gently, she slid her hand under the kitten's belly, still talking to it. "You're gonna love your new bed. It's all pink and soft."

The kitten didn't squeal at all as she lowered it down beside Misty.

One by one she moved the other three, talking to them, handling them so gently that not one cried.

Meg watched in growing amazement. How did Annie know how to be so skillful and gentle? She felt a flush of shame that the one she'd moved had been the only one that squealed.

Annie picked up the basket by its handle and carried it to the corner between the head of her bed and the outside wall. "There," she said. "They'll be right beside me."

"Okay," Meg said. "We need to get these wet sheets off your bed, and it's time for you to get dressed.

Annie was still in her little white nightgown, her curls tumbled. Looking at her, Meg's heart ached with tenderness.

She turned away and pulled the sheets off the bed. She'd hoped only the bottom sheet was stained, but they both were. She sighed. She hated washing sheets in the gray tubs behind the house. It made her back hurt. She felt the tension rising again, the headache threatening.

No. Calm down, she told herself. It's not worth a headache. She took a deep breath and gathered up the sheets.

After she and Annie had put clean sheets on the bed and she'd given the children breakfast, she started to work on the cake. Donny had gone off to play with Jack again, and Annie was upstairs adoring her kittens.

Five kittens, Meg thought as she put out cake ingredients on the counter. Why did she have to have five? Usually a young cat having her first litter had only two, maybe three. Misty was going to be hungry feeding all of them, and they were almost out of cat food. To say nothing of being almost out of people food. She'd have to use the last of the milk for the cake. She hoped it would come out all right. She'd never made a cake before. Nellie had made the children's cakes the year before, and before that Jesse had had a job and there was plenty of money for her to just go to the bakery and buy a cake.

Well, she told herself, I'm an intelligent woman with a college degree. I can certainly follow directions in a cookbook.

She set to work, but couldn't get the kittens off her mind. She'd have to find homes for them. She certainly couldn't have six cats running around underfoot, even if Jesse did get the job at Boston University.

She didn't know anyone in this podunk borough. How would she find homes for five kittens? And what would she do if she couldn't find homes for them?

Annie sat on the floor in the narrow space between her bed and the outside wall gazing into the basket at Misty and her kittens. She reached in and stroked Misty's head. "Mama said you're a really good mother. 'Course, you are. You're the best kitty in the world. And your babies are beautiful. They don't look like rats."

Annie bent to look at them closer. Donny had said that their eyes would open and their ears would perk up. She wondered how long that would take. Now there were just little lines where their eyes should be and their ears were little flaps close to their heads. She wondered why they came out that way.

How did they get out of Misty, anyway? She'd have to ask Mama.

Misty was licking them. Quite roughly, Annie thought. "Be gentle, Misty," Annie said. Misty kept on licking. She worked each kitten over from head to foot, licking so hard their little bodies rocked, but they didn't seem to mind. Annie knew she was washing them. She'd watched Misty wash herself lots of times. She could lick herself all over, sticking her hind leg up in the air and even licking her bottom. Annie sure couldn't do that.

As Misty cleaned the kittens, the colors in their fur showed more clearly. One of the yellow ones was yellow all over, a bright pretty yellow like a buttercup, that flower Mama would put under her chin to see if she liked butter. The other yellow one had orange stripes like a tiger.

I could name him Tiger, Annie thought. I could name all the kittens. They could have names like Misty does.

A thrill went through her. This was fun. Much more fun than naming her dolls, who were only pretend alive.

She would name the other yellow one Buttercup.

"I'm going to name your babies," she told Misty. Misty was still working over one of the gray kittens and didn't look up.

Gently Annie touched the tiger kitten. "Your name is Tiger," she told it. Then she laid her fingertip on the all-yellow one. "Your name is Buttercup."

Misty finished her licking and lay down on her side. The kittens crawled to her and pushed their faces against her tummy, searching for her nipples. Annie watched as one after the other latched on and started sucking, pushing their tiny paws against Misty's belly on either side of the nipple. Misty laid her big paw across them, stretched out, and began to purr.

Head tilted to one side, Annie studied the unnamed kittens. One of the gray ones was light gray like Misty. Annie leaned back on her hand just under the side of her bed and touched something soft. A ball of dust. Mama called them dust kitties. That was it! Annie touched the light gray kitten. "Your name is Dusty."

Three of them named. The other gray kitten was dark gray. It was a little bigger than the others and wiggled its tiny body as it nursed. "What shall I name you?" she asked it. Just then the factory whistle blew. Annie remembered looking down on the factory from her high place on the cliff and at the dark smoke coming out of its smoke stacks. The dark gray kitten was almost that color.

Annie hunched her shoulders in delight. With the tip of her finger she touched the dark gray kitten. "Your name is Smokey."

The only kitten that didn't have a name now was the one that was mixed yellow and gray. Annie looked at it more closely. It had gray and yellow in patches all over its body and a yellow smudge on its nose that Annie found especially endearing.

"We could call it Patches," Annie said to Misty. "But Patches isn't a very pretty name, and this is a specially pretty kitty."

Mama came into the room. "How are the kittens doing?"

Annie jumped up and ran to her mama. "They're doing fine. They're all nursing. And I'm naming them. I've got them all named but one. Come see."

Annie tugged on Mama's hand and looked up into her face.

Uh, oh. Mama had that look on her face. Annie had done something wrong. She let go of Mama's hand and drew back. Her tummy tightened. She was right near her bed. She could go under.

Mama stood still. Annie heard her draw in her breath and let it out again. Then she spoke. It was her gentle voice.

"What did you name them?"

Annie lifted her eyes to her mama's face. Mama looked sad but not mad. Annie's body softened.

"Do you want to see?"

"Yes." Mama sat down on the edge of the bed where she could look into the basket.

Annie took a big breath and went to the side of the basket, pointing as she named each kitten and told Mama how she found the names.

"I don't have a name for this one yet," she said, "but I think she's the prettiest of them all. I love the little yellow spot on her nose. The gray and yellow are like leaf shadows and sunshine, but I can't think of a name for her."

Mama had an odd look on her face, but it wasn't a mad look.

"Leaf shadows and sunshine make a dappled affect," she said.

"What does 'dappled' mean?"

"Different colors mixed together, like leaf shadows and sunshine, as you said."

"Dapple is a pretty word." Annie touched the gray and yellow kitten. "Your name is Dapple." She looked up at her mama, joy rising in her like a bubble. "Now they all have names."

"Yes. And I've come to tell you your lunch is ready."

"Can we have tuna fish again?"

"No, the tuna's all gone, but I've made you a peanut butter sandwich and we have more carrot sticks."

Annie was disappointed. She was sick of peanut butter, but she didn't say anything. She bent over the basket.

"Good-bye Misty. Bye Smokey and Dusty and Buttercup and Tiger and Dapple."

Then she took her mama's hand and went downstairs to lunch.

She's naming them, Meg thought with dismay. She's totally attached already. I never should have let her sit up there with them all morning. It'll be hell to persuade her to give them away when the time comes. *If I'm even able to find homes for them.*

"Come sit down now," she said to Annie.

Annie came to her place at the table and picked up her peanut butter sandwich. Meg could see she wasn't thrilled with it, but she was clearly hungry and didn't complain. She really was a good little girl. Donny was having lunch at Jack's again, getting at least one good meal for today. She should call Jack's mother, Ada was her name, and thank her, but she felt embarrassed that she didn't have enough food to invite Jack over in return.

As she and Annie ate, Meg's thoughts returned to the kittens. What interesting names Annie had chosen for them. Tiger, of course, from her picture books, but all the other names drawn from her sensitive awareness—buttercups and factory smoke, dust kitties, leaf shadows and sunshine. She had the makings of a poet.

Meg was pleased with her cake. It had come out perfectly and was now cooling in the pantry. She'd frost it while Annie was having her nap. Sugar was rationed because of the war, of course, but she'd been saving up coupons for a while and had enough to buy some sugar a few days ago.

Nellie had sent a doll for Annie's birthday. Meg was planning to tell Annie it was from everyone in the family, including Grandma and Aunt Nellie. She was grateful to Nellie that Annie could have a nice gift. Donny was making something for her, too. And Jesse had written that he would call that evening.

Never mind the kitten worry now. She just wanted Annie to have a good birthday.

They'd been eating a while in silence. Meg glanced over at Annie. She was frowning slightly, the way she did when she was trying to figure something out.

"Mama," she said suddenly. "How did Misty's babies get out of her tummy?"

Oh, my, Meg thought. Here it comes. Jesse had told her to always answer the children's questions; but in her family, no one would even dare ask such a question.

"Well..." Meg hesitated. "She pushed them out through a hole she has under her tail."

"Her b.m. hole?"

"No, another one, right beside the b.m. hole."

"She pushed them out like I do my b.m.?"

"Yes, sort of like that."

"Maybe that's why their ears are so flat." Annie seemed to consider for a moment, then asked, "Did you push me out of your tummy that way?"

Meg had told her a while back, in answer to other questions, that she had been in Meg's tummy before she was born.

"Yes." Meg pressed her lips together. What next?

"I'm gonna be a mama someday. Do I have a special hole for pushing babies out?"

"Yes." Meg's shoulders tightened. This business of answering the children's questions honestly could get out of hand.

"Where?" Annie put her heels up on the edge of the chair, lifted her skirt, and tried to look down between her legs. Of course, she couldn't see what she wanted, so she put her hand down to investigate.

That was too much for Meg. "Don't touch there," she said sharply. "That's not nice."

Annie pulled her hand away. Meg caught a glimpse of her frightened eyes before she lowered them. Instantly Meg regretted her sharpness. How could Annie pull so far away without even moving? Like a sea anemone that contracts at the slightest touch.

But what can I do? she asked herself. I can't have her poking around down there, stimulating herself. That's a recipe for an unwanted pregnancy in ten years. She sighed and tried to soften her voice.

"It's okay, Annie. You didn't know. Go wash your hands now before you touch your food again."

Annie obediently got up from the table, went to the kitchen, pulled the stool up to the sink, and washed her hands. When she came back to the table, she kept her eyes lowered and didn't ask any more questions.

Chapter Two 41

Annie lay quietly in her bed as dusk deepened, watching the leaves in the tree outside her window moving in the light evening breeze.

Her new doll lay beside her where Misty usually slept. Misty was in the basket with her kittens. Annie missed her, but she was so happy about the kittens that she didn't mind. Dolls were nice, but nowhere near as good as kitties. And now Annie had six kitties. That was the best birthday present of all.

Her tummy was full. Donny was right. Mama had made her a cake with five candles on top and even let her have two pieces. And she'd gotten two presents—the doll and a necklace Donny had made for her with blue and yellow beads from Mama's bead and button box.

Mama had been gentle almost all day, except for the time Annie had looked for her baby hole. She didn't know why she'd upset Mama then, or why she had to go wash her hands. Misty *licked* her baby hole. Annie had watched her doing it after lunch, with her hind leg up in the air.

Annie sighed. It was so hard to know what the wrong things were.

But still she was happy. Daddy had called, a special long-distance call. They couldn't talk long, because it was so expensive, but she'd told him about the kittens and he'd sung her the happy birthday song. She loved how he sang. And he said he'd be coming home soon. Maybe he wasn't like the daddy cat after all.

Annie leaned over the side of the bed to admire her kitties. Misty was stretched out on her side and all the kittens were nursing.

Each one was so special. Mama had said you couldn't tell yet if they were boys or girls, but she had decided Dapple and Buttercup were girls and Tiger and Smokey and Dusty were boys. She loved the way Tiger's orange stripes made his yellow even brighter. He would grow up to be like that poem Mama read to her— "Tiger, tiger burning bright." And Buttercup's yellow was really like a buttercup. Dusty's fur was exactly the color of Misty's, so soft and light, and Smokey's dark gray fur had an almost blue tint to it. Dapple was her favorite with the sweet little yellow smudge on her nose.

Annie wondered what color their eyes would be when they opened. She imagined Tiger's would be yellow and Dusty's green like Misty's. Did kitties ever have blue eyes like Annie's? She couldn't wait to see.

Annie stroked Misty's head and lightly touched each kitten. They were so tiny and fragile. Annie promised herself she would take really good care of them and never let anything bad happen to them.

"Goodnight, Misty," she said softly. "Goodnight Dusty and Buttercup and Tiger and Smokey and Dapple." Then she curled up and went to sleep to the sound of Misty's purring.

Chapter 3

"I need two more rocks that size," Donny said.

It was the day after Annie's birthday. Annie and Donny were up in the woods working on the fort. Annie had begged Mama to let her go alone, but Mama wouldn't. Then Annie had tried to persuade Donny to go exploring, not to her cave—that was secret—but somewhere new. But all Donny wanted to do was work on his stupid fort.

Annie stood still with the trowel in her hand. It was hot and she was tired. She looked up at the faint trail that led to her cave. She wanted to go to her cave again, but even more she wanted to go home and look at her kittens.

"I don't want to dig up any more old rocks," she said. She dropped the trowel.

"Aw, come on, Annie. I just need two more to finish this wall."

"I don't want to. I'm going home." Annie turned and started down the path. She hardly ever said no when Donny wanted her to do something, but she was really, really sick of digging up rocks.

She began to run. She was almost home when she heard a sound that made her run faster—the high, piercing squeak of a kitten in distress. What was happening? It sounded as if the cry were coming from her back yard. The kittens were supposed to be safe in their basket upstairs in her room.

She came to the end of the path and saw her mama standing by the rain barrel with Annie's kittens in her hands. They were squealing loudly. What was Mama doing with the kittens? Was she squeezing them?

Mama took the cover off the rain barrel and plunged one of the kittens into the water. Annie gasped, torn in two. She wanted to dash down into the yard screaming, "Mama, NO! NO! Don't hurt my kittens!" But her body was immobilized, her voice strangled in her throat, her mouth frozen open with the scream she couldn't utter.

Eyes wide with horror, she saw Mama hold the kitten down in the rain barrel a long, terrible moment, then toss its little body into the trash can. She plunged another kitten into the rain barrel. Its piercing cry was cut off. Annie had stopped breathing. One kitten still squealed. Then Mama held the last one down in the water, and all was silent.

Mama tossed two more little bodies into the trash can. She straightened, replaced the lids on the trash can and the rain barrel, wiped her hands on her apron, and went inside. She did not look up the hill or see Annie.

For a long moment, Annie stood paralyzed. Then her breath came back with a searing gasp. She tore across the yard to the trash can, pulled off the lid.

Three tiny bodies lay on top of waste paper and garbage. Annie pulled them out.

She crouched down on the ground behind the trash can and cradled them in her hands. Smokey, Dapple, and Tiger. Wet and still. Their last cries still echoed inside Annie, piercing her heart. Maybe they weren't all the way dead. Maybe if she held them and warmed them against her, they would wake up. They had to. They couldn't be dead. They'd been so warm and alive when she'd left them that morning to go up in the woods. She held them against her chest, but they didn't stir.

Sobs surged up in her, swiftly constricted by panic. Where were Dusty and Buttercup? Maybe Mama had gone to get them and kill them, too.

Annie scrambled to her feet, clutching the tiny wet bodies.

She had to get to Dusty and Buttercup before Mama did. She peered through the screen door. Mama wasn't in the kitchen. It took two hands to close the screen door without a sound. Annie had three pockets in her overalls. She tucked Dapple in her breast pocket, Tiger and Smokey into her side pockets and slipped silently through the back door. Her heart was racing and pounding so hard she could barely breathe.

She tiptoed through the kitchen. Mama wasn't in the dining room. Silently she went through and into the little square hall at the bottom of the stairs. Pressing herself against the wall, she peeked into the living room. Mama wasn't there either. Maybe she was already in the bedroom upstairs getting the other two kittens. Annie ran up the stairs. She would stop her Mama. She would kick her in the shins until she dropped the kittens. Then Annie would grab them and run.

The door to Mama's room was shut. She never shut it unless she was inside. Maybe … Annie caught a ragged breath. Mama wasn't in Annie and Donny's room. Annie ran to the corner where the basket was. Misty was lying inside, curled around Dusty and Buttercup.

Annie dropped to the floor with a sob of relief. But she must run, quickly, quickly, silently, before Mama came out of her room. She must take the basket and run. Where could she go?

Her cave.

When Annie picked up the basket, Misty jumped out. "Come, kitty, kitty." Annie whispered to her. Mama's door was still shut. Annie ran down the stairs, quietly, quietly, but the basket bumped once against the railing. Misty followed her, out through the dining room. In the kitchen Annie heard Mama's footsteps overhead. She was coming down.

If Annie could just get to the woods. The basket was bulky and bumped against her legs. She pushed through the back door so fast it slammed behind her. Across the yard and up the hill she ran with all her might, Misty a gray streak running beside her.

Meg sat hunched on her bed, her face pressed between her drawn-up knees.

The adrenalin of her impulsive action had drained out of her, and now she felt sick. How could she have drowned three baby kittens?

She'd been desperate. That was the problem. She shouldn't act out of desperation. There were always many options. She'd flipped into the worst one possible.

The mail had come early that morning, and still no check from Jesse. He'd told her he would send money from his tutoring. Every day she watched for it, and every day —nothing. She had only twenty-seven dollars and fifty-three cents left. They were out of milk and bread and almost out of peanut butter, and everything else as well. To replenish her basic stores would take almost all the money. She'd put off going to the grocery store hoping each day a check would come. She wanted to buy some more tuna fish and some apples. The children needed fruits and vegetables. She made them dig dandelion greens out of the miserable front lawn, but they protested. It was hard work and they didn't like dandelion greens. Meg knew they were bitter this time of year, but they were food.

The children were up in the woods. Annie had begged to go alone again, but Meg had refused. She'd told Annie she could go with Donny or not at all. She just didn't feel Annie was safe alone.

Meg had been down in the kitchen assessing the food situation when Misty had come winding around her legs and meowing to be fed. Insatiable cat. But of course she was hungry, nursing five kittens. The cat food was almost gone. How could she spend money on cat food when she couldn't feed her children?

There were too many kittens.

She had just snapped, dashed upstairs, grabbed three kittens, and drowned them. The sound of their cries came back to her, the feel of their little bodies struggling in her hand and then going still. Nausea swirled in her belly.

Annie would be devastated. She had named them all so poetically. Meg didn't even know which three she had grabbed. She hoped she hadn't drowned Dapple, who was clearly Annie's favorite.

What could she do now? She uncurled and sat on the edge of the bed. She could always think more clearly with her feet on the floor. Jesse had taught her to take deep breaths when she was upset. She pressed her feet into the floor and took three long breaths.

She'd tell Annie the kittens had died. That was it. Newborns did die sometimes. She shouldn't have thrown them in the trash can. She'd better go right away and get them before the children came back. She'd dry the kittens off and put them in a nice box with a scrap of old towel under them, and they'd do a funeral and bury them in the back yard. Annie would be sad, but she still had two kittens. She'd get over it.

She was just standing up to get the kittens from the trash can when she heard a soft thump on the stairway. She was suddenly hyper aware. What was that? Both children were up on the hill. Maybe it was Misty, but Misty usually moved silently. She'd better check.

As she hurried down the stairs, she heard the back screen door slam. Trepidation she dared not name surged through her. She strode through the dining room and the kitchen and stepped out into the yard.

With a final dash, Annie reached the thicket and ducked down behind it. Just in time. Mama came out the back door. She was tall and dark. She stood looking up the hill. Horror paralyzed Annie again. Could Mama see her? Misty crouched beside her. She seemed to know she had to be still. The kittens were quiet in the basket.

Annie watched in growing terror as Mama turned to the trash can, lifted the lid, and searched inside. Now she would know that the kittens were gone. She would know for sure that Annie had taken them. Annie felt them wet in her pockets.

Mama went inside.

Crouched in the thicket, stiff with fear Annie felt as if she couldn't move. But she had to. She must run, quickly, quickly before Mama found out the basket was gone, too. She scrambled to her feet.

Making sure to stay out of sight of the house, she pushed through the underbrush. It was hard to get the big basket through the bushes. It kept getting caught in vines and brambles. Annie's hands trembled as she worked to pull it free. Finally she came to a place where the path to the fort curved into the trees and was safe. It was easier running on the path.

She had almost reached the clearing where the fort was when she heard Donny banging rocks around and whistling Yankee Doodle. She'd forgotten that Donny would be there. He mustn't see her. But she had to go by the fort to find the trail that led to her cave.

She hesitated at the edge of the clearing. Her legs were trembling. Run! run! run! they urged her. She stepped backward and tripped on a stone that broke loose and crashed into the underbrush.

Donny was there in a second. "Annie, what're you doing?" He stood in front of her frowning. "Why're you taking the kitten basket up in the woods?"

Annie didn't know what to say. She couldn't tell Donny she was running away; he would just make her go home again. Her tongue stuck in her mouth. Then words came out without her thinking. "I'm taking the kittens for a walk."

"You're nuts. You're not supposed to go in the woods without me. Mama said so. And Mama wouldn't like you dragging her good basket through the bushes. You better go home right away before she knows."

Annie sidestepped along the edge of the clearing, her eyes darting back and forth to find the faint opening that was the trail to her cave. Donny was watching her. There was the trail. A few more quick steps and she ducked into it.

The basket caught on a dead branch sticking out from the overhanging tree. Donny was beside her grabbing her arm.

Fear and anger gave her strength. In one move, she yanked the basket free with a ripping sound and twisted her arm out of Donny's grasp.

"Leave me alone," she yelled at him, and turned and dived into the little trail, bending low under the branches.

Donny started to follow her. A branch she had pushed aside lashed back across his face. "Ow!" he yelled. The sound of his pursuit ceased. She pushed on, dragging the basket, bending low.

"You better go home," Donny shouted after her. "Mama'll be real mad. She'll kill you."

Annie caught back a sob. She crouched low, scrambling up the little trail as fast as she could away from Donny and his terrible words. She was no longer running. She couldn't. She had to duck under the overhanging branches and pull the basket through the narrow places. It got stuck again.

Annie dropped to the ground. Her heart was pounding so hard it felt as if her ribs would break. She remembered the way she had gone before, how narrow the path was, how she'd had to push through the bushes by the meadow where she had seen the deer.

It was too hard with the basket. She'd have to take the kittens out and carry them. The kittens seemed to be sleeping in spite of all the bumping. Carefully, carefully, she lifted out the pink towel and wrapped it around the kittens.

Misty was beside her. She looked up at Annie with an inquiring meow.

"It's okay," Annie told her. "The basket is too big to carry. We have to go to the cave. We'll be safe there."

Then she saw that there was a rip in the basket. It must have happened when she'd jerked it free from the dead branch, when Donny was grabbing her arm.

Mama's special basket. Mama would be so mad. She would yell at Annie and shake her and hit her really hard. Annie's cheek still hurt from the last time Mama had hit her. With a wave of nausea, Annie remembered her dream. Maybe Mama really was a witch, just pretending sometimes to be a gentle mama. Only a witch would kill little babies.

Cold terror ran through her. Annie and Misty and the kittens would never be safe to go home again.

Trembling all over, she finished folding the towel around the kittens, making a sort of pocket so the kittens wouldn't fall out. One of the kittens squealed.

"Hush, hush!" Annie told it. "We have to be very quiet."

Misty came close, sniffed the towel, and gave a soft purring meow. The kitten quieted.

Annie gathered the pink towel with the two tiny kittens close against her heart. She got to her knees, then to her feet, holding the folded towel in the curve of one arm. She needed the other hand to move the branches aside.

Slowly she went now, carrying her precious burden, agonizingly aware of the other three kittens, wet and still, in her pockets. The pain of that was so sharp she couldn't let herself feel it, but she could feel the wetness that had soaked through her overalls and T-shirt onto her skin. Even that sensation she pushed aside. She just needed to get the others to safety.

A little farther on, she came to the meadow where she had seen the deer. She stopped and remembered the mama deer and the young ones leaping over the bush, remembered lying on the grass and seeing the sky touching the trees and at the same time far away. Something softened and strengthened in her. She was a mama now. She had to take good care of her babies.

Meg looked all around. The yard was empty. She glanced up toward the woods, but saw nothing amiss. Maybe the door hadn't been latched and had banged in the wind. Only there wasn't any wind.

Never mind. She'd come to get the kittens out of the trash. She lifted the lid to the trash can. There were no kittens inside. She froze, staring at the tumble of trash and garbage. They must be there. She'd thrown them in there no more than fifteen minutes ago.

She reached in and stirred the refuse. No tiny, wet bodies. Slowly she straightened. Where could they have gone? Had one of the children taken them?

Her head began to pound. Realization poured through her like burning acid. If one of the children had taken them, then one of the children must have seen her drowning them. Had it been Annie? The thought was too unbearable to hold. Her mind veered away from it.

She suddenly had to know which kittens she had drowned. She turned and ran back into the house, ran up the stairs, and into the children's room. The corner by Annie's bed was empty.

Meg stood stunned. In a frenzy she whirled around, looked in the closet, under the bed, under Donny's bed.

Her brain spinning, she sank down on the edge of Annie's bed. Donny wouldn't have taken the basket. Only Annie would have. Annie who had seen her drowning the kittens and fearful that Meg would kill them all. She had taken the basket and run. That was the thump on the stairway and the banging of the screen door.

Where would she go but the woods? She couldn't have gone far.

Meg was on her feet, running back down the stairs. She grabbed the bell from the kitchen counter and dashed out into the yard, ringing long and loud. Surely Annie hadn't had time to go so far she wouldn't hear it. Donny would come.

Meg's head pounded. The sound of the bell was excruciating. She turned back into the house, set the bell carefully on the counter and dropped into a chair in the dining room. She laid her pounding head on her arms on the table.

If Annie had seen …

A short while later the screen door banged and Donny appeared beside her.

"What do you want, Ma? It's not even lunch time."

"Where's Annie?"

"She's up in the woods."

"I told you to keep her with you."

"I did, but she got tired of working on the fort, said she was going home to look at her kittens. I thought that was okay. But just a little while ago she came back. She had the kitten basket and was acting kind of funny. Like she was scared. I told her she had to go home, but she ran away into the bushes."

Meg felt rage rising in her. She stood up. "You let her go?"

Donny backed away out of reach. "I tried to stop her. I grabbed her but she yanked away and dove into the bushes. She didn't hold the branch like Dad taught us to, and it came back and hit me in the face. See?" He put his hand up to a red mark across his brow. "I think it's bleeding."

Meg clenched her teeth. She felt her right arm lifting to strike. Battling with the rage and headache, she froze, her arm poised in midair. Two long breaths. Slowly, she lowered her arm. It was no use anyway. Donny always dodged her blows. She sucked in three quick breaths, let out a long exhale.

"It isn't bleeding," she managed to say. "But it looks like it hurts."

Another breath. "Donny, I need you to help me. Go back right away. See if you can find Annie and bring her home. Please. It's important."

She could see Donny gauging her rage level, deciding that for the moment it was safe.

"Okay, Ma. I'll go. I'll try real hard to find her."

As he passed by her on the way out of the room, he gave her arm a quick pat. The arm she had lifted to strike him, that now lay limp at her side.

※

Holding Buttercup and Dusty close in the pink towel, Annie pushed through the bush the deer had jumped over and found the trail that went on from there. It was a longer way than she remembered, but at last she came to the open space and the steep slope that led up to the cliff. There beside the top of the cliff was her tree, standing tall and dark green against the sky.

Far below she heard the sound of Mama's bell. She was calling Annie and Donny home. A lump came in Annie's throat. She couldn't go home. She had to keep the kittens safe.

The last ascent to the base of the cliff was hard. It, too, was longer and steeper than Annie remembered. She was really tired. It was hot and she was hungry. It was almost lunch time, and she hadn't thought to bring any food.

A seed of despair sprouted in her heart. Where could she get food? Still she pushed on, trudged up the steep slope, scrambled up through the undergrowth beside the cliff on her knees and one hand, the other arm holding the pink towel with Dusty and Buttercup safe inside.

At last she came to the tree, and crept under its great sheltering branches. Underneath, the light was dim, the spruce needles soft under her knees. She made her way to the center where she could stand. Across the wide circle of spruce branches she could see her cave. She went to it, laid the pink towel down inside, and opened it. The kittens moved, blindly seeking their mother. One let out a squeak. Misty jumped onto the towel. She licked her kittens thoroughly, then lay down beside them. Annie let out a huge sigh.

At last they were safe in her cave.

※

Limp and spent, Meg lay on her bed listening for Donny to come back. The headache was easier now, since she'd vomited and wept. But she didn't know, couldn't begin to think, what she could say to Annie.

If only Jesse were here. Maybe she could call him. The phone bill wouldn't come in until later. Just to hear the sound of his voice. He would be angry at her, but he would know what to do. Maybe he could come home somehow, find enough gas coupons or take the train.

She rolled over and got up off the bed. Maybe Donny had found Annie by now. She hurried downstairs to the kitchen, leaned over the sink to look out the window, and searched the opening in the woods that led to Donny's fort. Several poison ivy vines with their clusters of three shiny leaves lurked near the opening to the path, mocking her. The edge of the sink pressed hard against her belly. After what seemed a long time, she heard him. Stones rattling ahead of him, the thump of his feet. He was as noisy as Annie was quiet.

He came into sight across the yard. Alone, but he had the basket in his hand.

Meg ran to the door to meet him. "Where's Annie?"

"Ma, I couldn't find her. I tried. I could see where she went through the bushes. I tracked her, like Dad taught me, but then I found the basket."

Meg realized she was clinging to the door frame.

"There were no kittens in the basket," Donny went on. "She must have taken them with her. And after I found the basket, I couldn't find her tracks anymore. Maybe her dragging the basket made her track clearer. I tried, Ma. I went pretty far. Maybe she'll come home when the noon whistle blows and it's lunch time. She's always hungry."

He handed Meg the basket. There was a long tear in its side. Already the edges of the tear were unraveling. It was irreparably damaged.

Annie sat watching Misty nurse Buttercup and Dusty. Only two kittens. She reached into her pockets and drew out three tiny bodies and laid them down on the pink towel next to Misty.

"Lick them," she said to Misty. "Maybe if you lick them, they'll come alive again."

Misty got up and smelled the kittens. She nudged Smokey with her front paw. He did not stir. Misty sniffed the kittens again. Then she picked up Dapple by the scruff of her neck and carried her out of the cave and over to the edge of the circle of spruce boughs. She dropped Dapple there, and went back to pick up Tiger and Smokey, one after the other, and carry them over to deposit them beside Dapple. Then she set to work with her front paws scratching spruce needles over the three limp kittens.

She was covering them up like she did her b.m., burying them. They must really be dead. Annie watched in anguish, her last spark of hope snuffed out. Grief rose up in her like a huge wave. Biting her lower lip, she drew in a long breath and held it for a long time.

Misty had gone back to the live kittens. If she was sad, she didn't show it.

Annie went and sat by the dead kittens. Misty had dumped them every which way and hadn't done a very good job of burying them. Annie brushed the spruce needles off them and laid them side by side. She stroked each one with the tip of her finger. Dapple, all sunshine and leaf shadows; Tiger with his fiery stripes who would never grow up to burn bright; Smokey with his deep blue-gray fur. Would his eyes have been blue like Annie's? Between the sobs that were welling up, she spoke to them.

"Now I'll never know what color eyes you have, or what you'll look like when your ears perk up. I was going to play with you, tie a piece of paper on a string and pull it so you could chase it. Misty has a little ball you could have run after; and when you were big enough to go outside, I was going to wiggle a stick in the grass for you to pounce on."

She had planned it all in the hours she sat adoring them, and now they were dead. The wave of grief rose higher, crashed over her and swept her under. Sobs held back in her desperate flight convulsed her. She lay down and curled around the dead kittens and cried until she was too exhausted to cry anymore.

Chapter 4

Meg couldn't bear to look at the ruined basket. She crossed the small kitchen and stuck it under the bottom shelf in the pantry. It couldn't be mended. Maybe she'd burn it in the furnace when the weather got cold.

She knew Annie would have been horrified to have torn her mama's special basket. Surely it had been an accident. But now Annie would be even more afraid to come home.

Donny had said she looked scared. Of course she was scared after seeing her mama drown her beloved kittens. What a terrible monster she must think her mother was. And she'd be heartbroken at seeing her kittens dead. Oh, what was she doing with those little, dead kittens she'd pulled out of the trash?

"Ma." Donny was standing by the back door, shifting from one foot to the other. "Can I go over to Jack's?"

She'd been so lost in her thoughts that she'd forgotten he was there. He looked uncomfortable. In spite of his boyish loudness and his ability to adapt, she knew he was almost as sensitive as Annie. Surely he felt Meg's anguish and confusion and wanted to escape. She glanced down at her watch. Eleven thirty. If he went now, they'd ask him to lunch. She had almost nothing to offer him here. She'd planned to go to the store that morning to use the last of her money to replenish the pantry—but then her crazy, impulsive act had turned everything upside down.

Donny was waiting. Meg hated him calling her Ma. It was so lower class. But Jesse had told her to leave it alone. He needed to fit in with his friends.

"May I," she corrected him. "Yes, you may. If they invite you for lunch, you may stay. Be sure and say thank you."

"'Course. I always do." He hesitated, shifting his weight again. "Ma, when Annie comes back, don't hit her." He looked straight into her eyes for a half second. Then he was out the back door with a bang. Meg heard the crunch of his bicycle tires on the gravel driveway as he sped away.

She stood with her hand pressed over her heart. "Don't hit her," he'd said. As if he knew she had hit Annie the last time she'd stayed up in the woods. Had Annie told him? Did they talk about things like that together? Or was it because he'd noticed the bruise on Annie's cheek? She remembered his eyes, so like Jesse's, blue, intense, and the flash of anger in the look he'd given her. Had Annie told him about the drowned kittens when they met in the woods? Did Donny know? She found she was trembling.

She was hungry, but there was next to nothing in the house. She looked in the pantry. Some dried beans. Some flour. A little sugar left over from frosting Annie's cake. Annie's cake, still half of it left. But she couldn't eat that. She was saving it for Annie. Some crackers. The almost empty jar of peanut butter.

Standing by the sink, still feeling shaky, she spread the rest of the peanut butter on some crackers and drank a glass of water. That would have to do. She really did need to go to the store. She wanted to have something good to give Annie when she came home. It was only a twenty-minute walk to the village. She could go and be back in an hour. But what if Annie came home and there was no one there? No, Meg would wait. Surely Annie would come home soon and they could go to the store together.

Meg realized she had been staring out the window at the path into the woods all the time she ate. How long would Annie stay up in the woods? Meg thought of the way that Annie ran and hid and froze when she was frightened. Jesse was best at coaxing her out, but Meg had managed it just the other day. How long would Annie hide if no one found and coaxed her?

She paced through the dining room and into the living room. She didn't know what to do with herself. There was plenty of work to do. The lawn needed mowing, but that was impossible in this heat. The stained sheets from Misty's birthing were still soaking in the washtubs out back. She hadn't cleaned the house for several weeks. But she couldn't begin on anything. All she could think of was Annie, alone up in the woods, carrying dead and alive kittens, grieving and full of fear.

She threw herself down on the living room couch and curled up, her arms wrapped around her head.

Annie woke, fuzzy and confused, to the sound of the three o'clock factory whistle. At first she didn't know where she was or what had happened to make her head and heart hurt so. Then, as her eyes focused, she saw the three dead kittens lying in the spruce needles beside her. Ants were crawling on them.

She sat up. "No," she said to the ants. "Get off my babies." She brushed at them, but they seemed determined to cling to the little dead bodies. She picked Dapple up to brush the ants off her. Dapple's tiny body was stiff. One of the ants crawled on Annie's hand and bit her.

"Ow!" Annie slapped at the ant. But she was more concerned about Dapple. What had made her body so stiff? Annie touched Tiger and Smokey and found that they had stiffened, too. As fast as Annie brushed them away, the ants came back. The sting on her hand hurt, and she felt like crying again. She didn't want her kittens to be stiff like that.

She looked over to the cave. Dusty and Buttercup were curled up together on the pink towel. Misty was nowhere in sight.

Maybe she'd gone hunting. Maybe she was hungry like Annie. Maybe she'd gone down to the house to ask Mama to feed her. Annie shivered. She remembered how Mama had looked the last time Annie had seen her, standing in the kitchen door, tall and terrible. What if Mama killed Misty? The thought was too raw to bear. If she didn't have Misty, she would be so sad she'd never stop crying. And then only Annie would be left to take care of Buttercup and Dusty.

Annie crawled to the cave and gently touched the two kittens. They were soft and warm, alive. They felt very different from the way Smokey and Dapple and Tiger felt.

Annie went back to the dead kittens and picked each one up. Smokey and Dapple and Tiger were really, really dead, stiff and cold in her hands. Maybe Misty had tried to bury them so the ants couldn't get them.

Annie started crying again, but even as she wept, she decided she must bury the kittens properly, not just with spruce needles.

She sucked up her tears. She needed the trowel that was down at the fort. But she couldn't leave the kittens. The pockets of her overalls had dried. Very gently, speaking softly to the kittens, she picked them up and tucked them both into her breast pocket. They didn't cry at all and didn't seem to mind being in such close quarters. Maybe it was like how they'd been in Misty's tummy.

This is how it feels to be a mama, Annie thought. Only I'm going to be a gentle mama and never hurt my babies.

She crawled out from under the tree and backed down the slope beside the cliff on her hands and knees, aware not to crush the precious burden in her pocket. She knew her way now, easily found the place at the bottom of the open space where her path into the woods began. With the kittens in her pocket, she could move more freely than she'd been able to coming up; and even though she'd passed there only three times, she'd moved aside enough branches and left enough tracks on the forest floor to make her trail clear. She soon reached what she had come to call the deer meadow, and went on through.

She came to the place where she had left the basket, but the basket wasn't there. She stiffened and gripped the branch above her. How could it not be there? Crouching down, she searched under the bushes. No basket, but in the soft earth, she saw her own footprints and other footprints. Donny's. He must have followed her after all, found the basket, and taken it back to Mama. Now she'd know that Annie had torn it. Annie felt sick. Mama would be so mad.

As she approached the fort, she slowed down, using all her skills of quietness to move silently. She didn't want to run into Donny again.

He wasn't there. The trowel lay where she had dropped it that morning. She picked it up and stood a moment in front of the fort, looking down the hill. Hunger cramped in her belly. Just a little farther down the path was her house, her bed, food. And sometimes a gentle mama who took care of Annie and sang her songs and told her stories and was teaching her to read.

But the gentle mama could turn into a witch at any time and kill Dusty and Buttercup. Annie remembered her dream, the feel of her mama's hands, like claws, on Annie's shoulders, the shaking, the slap the day Annie first found the cave. Now Annie had torn Mama's special basket. She couldn't go back.

Annie sucked up the sobs that threatened and wiped her nose on the shoulder of her shirt. She had to be strong. Trowel in hand, she was just turning to go back up the hill into the trees when she saw Misty bounding toward her up the path from the house. In a moment, Misty was winding around her legs and talking to her with her special purr meow.

Joy and relief poured through Annie. She bent and gathered Misty up into her arms. "Oh, Misty, I'm so glad to see you. I was scared Mama would hurt you. Did you go home? Did Mama feed you?"

Misty was busy investigating the kittens in Annie's pocket. She sniffed each one and gave them each a lick, then wiggled to get down. As soon as she touched the ground she started down the path toward the house, her tail in the air. She looked back at Annie with an imperative meow that seemed to say, "Let's go home now. We've had enough adventures. Let's go home where it is safe and comfy."

"No, Misty, we can't," Annie told her. "It *isn't* safe. We have to go back to the cave."

She turned to the trail that led into the woods, looking back over her shoulder. "Come, kitty, kitty," she called. Misty hesitated, then followed her.

It was hot, even under the shade of the trees. Annie trudged up the hill, bending under the branches, pushing through the thickets. It was harder going up hill, and seemed a long way. When at last she came to the open space below the cliff, she saw that the sun was lower in the sky, dropping toward the hill, and the tree shadows were longer.

A flutter of fear stirred in her heart. Night would come. She pushed the thought away, but the flutter of fear stayed with her as she climbed the last bit to the base of the cliff, crawled up the side and under the branches of her tree.

She went to the cave, lifted the kittens out of her pocket and laid them on the pink towel. They mewed as she moved them. Misty, who had been following close behind Annie, went to them and lay down to nurse them.

Annie stroked Misty's head. "I'm so glad you came back with me. I need you to feed my babies. I need you … to be with me."

It was time to bury the dead kittens. Annie went to where they lay, covered with ants again. Where should she bury them? Maybe this place that Misty had chosen would be right. It was still under the tree, but near the edge of the circle where the branches touched the ground.

Annie pulled away spruce needles next to the place where the dead kittens lay. Then she found the trowel where she had laid it near the mouth of the cave and began digging.

Chapter Four

The soil was hard and dry and stony. Annie'd had lots of practice digging up rocks for Donny, but still it was hard work. It took her a long time to make a hole she thought was deep enough.

She picked up the little bodies, stiff and cold and still, brushed the ants off them one last time, and laid them side by side in the hole.

"Good-bye Smokey, good-bye Dapple, good-bye Tiger," she said. She gathered loose dirt in her hand and spread it over them. Her sadness felt unbearable. She began to cry again as she laid more dirt over her dead babies. Still she worked, her tears falling on the little grave until all the dirt was back in the hole and patted down.

She sat back on her heels, tears still pouring down. All at once her grief flipped to rage.

"I hate you, Mama," she cried out between her sobs. "I hate you. You call me wicked, but I'm not wicked like you. I don't hit people and scream at them, and *I don't kill babies.* You're the wicked one. I hate you."

She threw herself down, pounding the ground, sobs tearing through her. Finally her sobs subsided. Exhausted she lay sprawled among the spruce needles beside the kittens' grave.

She stretched out a hand and touched it. The grave needed a stone on it. She rolled and sat up. She remembered going with Grandma and Aunt Nellie to visit Grandpa's grave, and Grandma telling her the stone was there with Grandpa's name on it so she and Aunt Nellie could come visit Grandpa and put flowers on his grave.

"I'm going to find a pretty rock for your grave," she told her lost kittens. "And I'll pick some flowers to put on it. Then later I'll come back and put fresh flowers on it, like Grandma does with Grandpa's grave."

Come back from where? The question rose inside her, and the fluttering panic that had been licking at the edge of her awareness rose to consciousness. Wasn't she going to stay here? But how could she? There was no food. Or water. Annie noticed that she was thirsty as well as hungry. And night would come.

In fairy tales, the children found roots and berries in the forest and fished in a stream and drank from the stream. But there was no stream in these woods and Annie hadn't seen any berries.

Pushing down her fear, Annie brought her attention back to the business of finding a gravestone. She crawled out from under the tree and walked around on the top of the cliff. There were lots of rocks scattered about, some of them with bits of mica in them, catching the late sunlight.

Annie thought of the little garden Mama had helped her make inside a round, glass vase. They'd put in moss for grass and little twigs for trees and a bit of mica for a lake. It was so pretty. Annie had loved it. When Aunt Nellie's birthday came, Annie gave her the little garden for a present.

A rock with mica would be perfect for the kittens' grave. Annie looked around and found just the right one.

She went to the edge of the cliff and looked down. Far below was the roof of her house, half hidden by the trees. The sight of the roof and the cramps of hunger in her belly tugged at her again. An urge rose up in her to gather up the kittens and run, run back down the hill to home and safety. There would be a drink of water and food. Even though there wasn't a lot of food, Mama always had something for them at mealtime.

But it wasn't safe.

She turned away from the cliff edge and looked at the stone in her hand. She needed to put it on the grave.

Dropping to her hands and knees, she crawled under the tree to the place where she'd buried the kittens. The spruce needles were disturbed around the grave. Annie spread them over the bare earth and placed the stone on top. A ray of sunlight slanted through the branches and glistened on the mica.

Now she needed to find some flowers. She crawled back out and walked across the top of the cliff. There were some blue cornflowers along the side opposite her tree and some wild sunflowers over at the edge of the woods.

Chapter Four

Meg woke with her head pounding. She sat up, stiff and achy from lying curled up so tightly. She glanced at her watch. Three thirty! She must have been asleep. What was she doing sleeping on the couch in the middle of the day?

Then all the events of the day came back to her in a sickening rush. Meg gave herself a little shake. Maybe Annie had come back while Meg was sleeping. She always moved so quietly Meg wouldn't have heard her. Maybe she was upstairs in her room. Meg got up and climbed the stairs.

There was no one in the children's room. No Annie asleep on the bed. No cat or kittens. Meg stood in the doorway feeling the emptiness of the room, her brief hope crushed.

Sorrow and fear welled up in her. Her mind pushed those emotions away. Annie *had* to come back. She'd be hungry. She hadn't had lunch. Surely she'd be back soon and they'd go to the store together and get something good for supper.

Maybe she should make a shopping list while she waited for Annie. She went down the stairs, thinking as she descended. She would get a chicken. There was probably enough money for that. She could roast it and they would have leftovers for several days. In the kitchen, she found a pad and pencil and began jotting.

A loud meow interrupted her concentration. Misty had her paws up against the screen door, asking to be let in. Misty! Then Annie must be on her way back. Meg dropped her pencil and rushed to the back door. There was no one in the yard, no Annie emerging from the woods. Meg stared up the path, willing Annie to come running toward her. The path stared back at her. Empty.

"Annie," Meg called. "Annie."

Misty was rubbing against her legs, demanding with increasingly insistent meows to be fed.

"All right, all right," Meg responded. "I'll give you what cat food is left. Then that's it. You'll have to catch some mice. Where is Annie? Why didn't you bring her with you?"

She turned back to the kitchen, opened the cupboard and poured the remaining cat food into Misty's dish. She watched Misty eat and felt her own hunger pangs. The peanut butter and crackers hadn't been near enough for her lunch. She picked up her pencil again but couldn't focus on a shopping list. Misty would go back to Annie and the kittens. If only Donny were here, Meg would make him follow Misty and bring Annie back. She shouldn't have let him go.

Misty ate quickly and then was at the back door asking to be let out. As soon as Meg opened the door, she ran across the yard and disappeared into the woods. She went so fast Donny couldn't have followed her, even if he had been there.

⁕

Annie decided to explore. Maybe she could find some berries in the woods. She'd pick flowers for the grave on the way back. As she started into the woods, she heard the factory whistle blow. It was the suppertime whistle. Annie stopped a moment, suddenly weak with hunger. She had to find some berries.

There was a patch of poison ivy right in front of her. She walked wide around it and came upon another animal trail like the one that had led her up from the fort. She bent under the overhanging branches and followed it. After only a short way, she came to a clearing, smaller than the deer meadow. She stopped at the edge of it.

There was a slight movement in the underbrush on the other side of the clearing. A fox emerged. Annie caught her breath. He had reddish fur, a pointed nose, and a long fluffy tail. He paused, one front paw lifted, and sniffed the air, turning his head slightly from side to side, then strolled across the clearing, his bushy tail a graceful arc behind him, and disappeared again into the trees.

A fox! Annie had never seen an alive fox before, but she'd seen a picture of one in her animal book. Mama always made sure Misty was inside at night because foxes could eat kitties.

What if the fox found Misty and the kittens? Annie turned in a flash, ran back through the animal trail, and arrived breathless at the top of the cliff.

The kittens weren't safe, even in the cave. Nowhere was safe. Annie must stay close to the cave and protect Misty and the kittens. She'd find a big stick and hit the fox with it if he came near.

Forgetting about flowers and berries, she looked around for a good stick. There weren't any lying on the ground, but there was a big, dead branch hanging from a tree at the edge of the woods near where the cornflowers grew. Annie went to it and tugged. It was broken from the bigger branch it was part of, but only half broken and didn't come loose. Annie tugged again. No use. She needed a knife. Daddy would have had a knife in his pocket and cut the branch free in a moment.

Annie didn't have a knife, but she had a trowel. She ran to her tree and crawled underneath. In the cave, Misty and the kittens were sleeping. The trowel lay nearby. Annie grabbed it and crawled out again.

She was moving fast, pushed by fear. She had to get the stick before the fox came.

The place where the branch was broken was almost as high as Annie could reach. She stood on her tip toes and hacked at the broken place with the side of the trowel. Hacked and tugged. The broken place looked a little more broken, but still her stick didn't let go. Annie reached up again and hacked with all her might. Then she dropped the trowel, grabbed the branch with both hands and jumped. The branch came loose all at once, and Annie fell backward onto the hard rock surface of the ledge, the branch clutched against her chest.

After Meg finished the shopping list, she decided to clean the living room. At least start. She could get the dusting done. She'd noticed that morning that dust was visible on the piano and the top of the bookcase.

Her hands were shaking as she picked up a dust rag and furniture polish from the pantry. Unwilling to admit to herself how upset she was, she hurried to the living room. She'd just get busy and do something useful.

There was a white doily on top of the bookcase, part of a set that Jesse's mother had given them for a wedding present. In the center was a delicate blue glass vase filled with wildflowers that Donny had brought her a few days before. As Meg moved to dust around the doily, her unsteady hand bumped the vase and sent it crashing to the floor. It landed between the bookcase and the rug, scattered flowers and water, and shattered into innumerable pieces.

"No!" Meg cried out. Her hands shaking even more, she knelt on the floor to gather up the pieces. There were myriad tiny fragments. She'd have to get the dustpan to sweep them up. She began to cry. Two of her beautiful treasures destroyed in one day. And Annie gone.

In that moment, as she wept over her broken vase, she knew with sudden surety that Annie would not come back on her own. She would be too frightened. She'd seen her mama drown her kittens, she'd torn her mama's basket, and she had stayed away all day when her mama had called her. Remembering how hard she had struck Annie only two days ago, Meg could barely imagine what Annie now feared.

Only Jesse would be able to find her and coax her out. Leaving the scattered glass and flowers on the floor, Meg got up and went to the hall. She should have called him sooner.

The phone hung on the wall opposite the bottom of the stairs. She reached out to pick up the receiver, then drew her hand back. If Jesse came home she'd have to tell him what she had done. He would be angry. He was rarely angry, and when he was, he controlled it well; but

Meg dreaded his anger. His love for her and his patience and kindness in spite of her storms were her lifeline. If he stopped loving her…

Maybe if Annie did come back on her own, Jesse would never need to know that Meg had drowned her kittens. Annie might be afraid to tell him. Then Meg could say, as she had planned to say to the children, that the kittens had just died.

No, she couldn't. She had promised Jesse never to lie to him. If she did and he found out, if Annie told him, he would never trust her again. Integrity was his highest value.

Standing by the phone, she wavered. She'd just clean up the broken vase, then decide what to do.

Moving automatically, she went to the pantry for the dustpan and brush. When all the glass was cleaned up, she carried it out to the trashcan in back. As she lifted the lid, a wave of nausea hit her. Only a few hours ago, she'd thrown three dead kittens in there—and Annie had seen.

She had to call Jesse. Nothing was more important than getting Annie safely home. She returned to the hall and picked up the receiver.

The operator's nasal voice came over the line. "Number please."

Trying to keep her voice steady—who knew how many gossips were listening in on the party line—Meg gave her the number of Jesse's brother. She heard the click of the connection, then the sound of ringing. It rang eight times.

"Doesn't sound like anyone's home," the operator commented.

"No. Thank you. I'll try again later."

Click.

Meg hung up the receiver.

She dropped down on the bottom step. Maybe she should ask someone local to help her. But who could she ask? She hadn't made any friends since she moved here. What could she talk about with factory workers' wives? The nearest neighbors were half a mile or more away.

She didn't know them at all, and Annie wouldn't come out of hiding for strangers anyway. There was no one she could call. Only Jesse could find Annie and coax her out of her hiding place.

What if she couldn't reach him?

Desperation unhinged her. Even knowing it was futile, she rushed to the kitchen, grabbed the bell from the counter, and banged out through the back door. The late afternoon sun had disappeared behind the trees and the shadow of the woods fell across the yard. Meg rang and rang until her arm ached, called and called, "Annie, Annie, come home."

Her voice faded into the thick silence under the trees. She was alone, alone. No one to help.

Annie lay on her back, stunned. Her head spun and hurt where she had banged it against the rocky floor of the ledge. She was looking up into the sky. Pink clouds floated above her. They were really, really pretty.

She turned her head and saw the trees on the hill above, green against the sky. She began looking again at how the leaves touched the sky and at the same time how far away the sky was.

That opposite things could both be true amazed her and seemed to tell her something she didn't yet understand but that gave her comfort. Maybe the sky was touching her, too. It felt as if it might be, coming right down and touching her face and chest even though she couldn't see it.

Her fall had knocked the urgency out of her. She had her stick. She lay thinking about the sky touching her and how comforting that felt.

Maybe the sky was God. Annie didn't know much about God. Daddy never spoke of him, but she knew Mama talked to him sometimes and asked him to help her be good.

Did Mama want to be good? That was a new idea for Annie. Mama must want to be good or she wouldn't ask God to help her. Then why did she hit Annie? That wasn't a good thing to do. She did it when Annie did something wrong.

But Annie never meant to do wrong things. She rolled over and sat up to think about it better. It was confusing. Annie tried all the time to be good. She wasn't wicked. "I'm not wicked," she said aloud, looking down from the cliff at the roof of her house far below.

If Mama wanted to be good, why did she kill the kittens? That was a wicked thing to do. Annie was sure about that. The thought of the dead kittens made Annie sad again.

She got up slowly. Her head was still spinning, but after a few steps she found her balance. She crossed the ledge and picked flowers to put on the grave—blue cornflowers for Smokey, orange sunflowers for Tiger, but for Dapple there were no flowers as magical as leaf shadows and sunshine. Annie picked a few leaves off an overhanging branch for Dapple.

The woods were shading the ledge now. Annie could see the shadows of the tops of the trees way down at the bottom of the open space, blending into the trees below.

Back under the spruce tree, she arranged the flowers and leaves on the grave, laid her stick near the entrance to the cave, and curled up close to Dusty and Buttercup and Misty, half in and half out of the cave.

As she settled down, she heard the whine of a mosquito around her head, then felt a sharp sting on her cheek. She twisted and slapped. When they went camping Mama always rubbed some stinky stuff on their skin to keep away mosquitoes. Annie didn't have any. Another whine and a sting on her arm.

Chapter 5

The phone rang. Meg uncurled out of the big chair where she had retreated with the *Ladies' Home Journal* and rushed to get it.

Maybe it was Jesse. Maybe he had somehow known she was trying to reach him. She snatched up the receiver and pressed it to her ear.

"Hello." It was a woman's voice. "This is Ada Martin, Jack's mom."

Meg couldn't speak.

"Hello?"

"Hello," Meg managed to answer.

"Donny just told us his sister is lost in the woods. He's quite worried about her. Has she come home yet?"

"No, not yet. I'm worried, too."

"Of course you are, poor dear. Look, Mike, my husband, gets off at the factory at six. It's five thirty now, so he'll be home soon. Why don't we come over? Mike and Donny and Jack can all go looking together. Mike's a good tracker. He can organize the boys and they'll find her for sure. Donny says she's only five. She can't have gone far."

Ada's voice was warm. Meg felt something let go inside her. "That … that would be very kind. Thank you."

"We'll be over soon then. We'll bring Donny when we come. Mike can throw his bike in the back of the truck. Don't you worry any more. We'll find her."

Meg hung up. She felt weak in the knees with relief. She wasn't alone after all. Someone was coming to help.

Uh oh. Was the house neat enough? She hurried into the dining room. The table needed wiping. In the kitchen, the empty cracker box, the peanut butter knife and the empty peanut butter jar cluttered the counter. Swiftly, she washed the knife, tossed the empty containers into the wastebasket under the sink, and wiped down the counter. Then she took the dish cloth into the dining room and gave the table a thorough scrub. In the living room, the dust rag and bottle of furniture polish lay on the floor where she had left them when she cleaned up the broken vase. Flowers were still scattered across the rug and the rug was wet. She gathered up the flowers, found an old towel and sopped up most of the water.

When all that was done, she decided she might as well finish the dusting. It would be a little while before the Martins arrived. Martin. That was their last name. She realized she knew nothing about them, had never talked to Ada to thank her for having Donny over almost every day. Well, she'd meet them soon. And it was very kind of them to come look for Annie. Maybe they'd find her. A wisp of hope fluttered up in her heart.

She'd just finished the dusting when she heard the roar of a truck arriving and the crunching of gravel as it stormed up the steep driveway.

Looking out the window, Meg saw a big, heavy-set man lifting Donny's bike out of the back of the truck. Donny, and another boy who must be Jack, climbed out of the back seat. Pushing his bike, Donny led Jack and his father around to the back of the house.

Ada came to the front door. Meg felt a rush of embarrassment. She hadn't closed the bathroom door at the top of the stairs.

But Ada wasn't looking up. "Hi," she greeted Meg with a wide smile. "I'm Ada."

She wore jeans and a stained, blue T-shirt. Her straight, brown hair was pulled back in a ponytail. Her face was round, her eyes round and blue, her cheeks rough and sunburned, and she carried a big black pot braced against her substantial abdomen.

"Hi," Meg answered. "I'm Meg." She held out her hand, then realized both Ada's hands were holding the pot. "Please come in."

"I made a stew this afternoon and brought you some," Ada said. "It's venison from Mike's hunting trips. We needed to clean out the deep freeze 'cause it's gonna be hunting season again soon. So I made a big stew, plenty to share. Where shall I put it?"

Meg couldn't believe how awkward she felt. She who had always been so socially graceful and charming. She was almost stammering. "Thank you so much. That's very kind. You shouldn't have."

"O' course I should've. When there's trouble, it's awful hard to think about cooking." She followed Meg into the kitchen. "Better put it on the stove. It's still hot."

A big pot of stew. Meg could hardly believe such bounty. Ada set the pot on the stove and lifted the lid. A rich aroma floated out. Meg's salivary glands sprang into action. She swallowed. "It smells delicious."

Ada beamed. "It's a good one. Lotsa vegetables in there, too. Now I've already fed the boys and Mike can eat later at home. This here's for you and your little girl."

Donny came in the back door, followed by Mike and Jack. The small kitchen was suddenly full of male energy.

Ada introduced them. "This is Jack and my husband, Mike. Donny's mom, Meg."

"Good to meetcha." Mike held out a big hand. Like a bear paw, Meg thought as she shook it. But there was something reassuring about Mike's size and strength and his deep gruff voice.

"Nice little place you got here," Mike commented, looking around. "Those trees come almost down to your house. Bet there's a bunch of deer up there on the hill."

"I imagine there are," Meg said. "I can't go up there myself."

"That's a shame," Ada said. "Donny told us as how you got sick from the poison ivy."

Chapter Five

What else has he told them? Meg wondered.

Donny came to stand close to her. Meg put her arm around his shoulders. "I want to thank you for having Donny over so often," she said.

Mike punched Donny lightly on his arm. "Donny's always welcome. He's a fine boy."

"And has such nice manners," Ada added.

Mike hitched up his belt. "Well, boys, we'd better get going. We got about an hour and a half of daylight left. Easier to find the little girl before it gets dark."

Meg squeezed Donny's shoulders. "Show them the path you found this morning."

Donny leaned against her for just a moment. "I will," he said, then followed Mike and Jack out the door.

"Let's sit down while we wait," Meg suggested to Ada. She was beginning to recover her social skills. "I think we'll be more comfortable in the living room."

They settled in the living room and visited, Ada in the big chair and Meg on the couch. Ada was quite talkative and told Meg a great deal about Woodsborough and the steel factory that employed almost everyone who lived there.

"They got a grip on the town, but they're caring of their workers," Ada told her. "They don't run the forge on Mondays so we wives can hang out our wash and not have it covered with soot. Guess you don't get so much of that out here, but in town it's something awful all the other days."

Meg found herself enjoying Ada's chatter. She'd been alone too much. But even as she listened, she felt her stomach growling and couldn't stop thinking about the stew on the stove. And as time passed, she found herself shifting on the couch, glancing at the windows, growing increasingly tense as twilight deepened outside.

Finally she stood up to turn on a light. "I hope they find her soon," she said. "It's getting dark. I'm going to turn on the backdoor light so they can find their way."

"Mike brought a big flashlight. They'll find their way okay."

"I hope they find Annie."

"They will."

※

Annie was far away in fantasy land. Elves had come to take her to their magic castle deep in the woods. They brought a basket for the kittens that was even more beautiful than Mama's special basket. When Annie looked inside, there were five kittens. Dapple and Smokey and Tiger weren't dead after all. That had just been a bad dream. The kittens had grown. Their ears had perked up and their eyes had opened and they were so cute and sweet that Annie's heart was bursting with love and delight.

The elves' castle was made of trees with big trunks. The roof of the castle was their branches, and there were little lights, like Christmas tree lights, all different pretty colors hanging among the leaves. All around the castle was a sparkling stream. The water was magic so when Annie drank from it, all her sadness and the ache in her cheek where Mama hit her went away. She wasn't scared anymore. She was safe. The elves said she and the kittens could stay forever. And they were bringing big plates of magic food—

A voice calling her startled Annie out of her fantasy. She wasn't in the elves castle anymore. She was under the spruce tree and it was getting dark. Mosquitoes whined around her. She was hungry and thirsty. Her cheek still ached, and there were only two kittens in the cave, still tiny with closed eyes and ears flat against their heads.

The voice calling her was a deep man's voice, but not Daddy's. Maybe it was a bad guy. Misty lifted her head, listening. Her eyes shone in the dim light.

"Shh," Annie whispered to her.

The man's voice called her name again. Annie's body crunched up with fear. Gripping her stick, she crawled to the edge of the circle of spruce boughs and peered through. Just below the cliff, in the open space without trees, stood a big man with black hair. He was scanning the top of the cliff. "Annie," he called again. "Come out. We've come to take you home."

Annie drew back, but not so far that she couldn't still see what was happening. Now the big man was looking around the sides of the cliff. Would he see the tunnel she'd made in the undergrowth where she'd crawled up and down beside the cliff? Annie held her breath, her heart pounding. The man came close to her tunnel, but just then Donny and another boy came bursting out of the trees below.

"Daddy, we found another trail," the boy said. "Come see."

The big man turned away and started down the hill toward the boy. Maybe he wasn't a bad guy after all. Maybe the other boy was Jack and that was Jack's daddy. Donny had told Annie that Jack's daddy was really nice and helped them build a tree house.

Donny stayed behind, looking up at Annie's tree. "Annie," he called. "You gotta come home now. Mama's really worried about you."

Annie drew farther back from the edge of the spruce boughs. Mama was worried and had sent Donny and Jack and Jack's daddy to hunt for her. If she came out they would take her home. But Annie knew only too well what Mama did when she was worried. She knew Mama wouldn't hit her in front of Jack's daddy, but after Jack's daddy left...

Annie saw her mama standing over the rain barrel, throwing the dead kittens into the trash, saw her face contorted with rage as she shook Annie and called her a wicked girl.

Her belly knotted in fear. She couldn't go home.

Donny still stood looking up at the tree, as if he knew she was there. "Please, Annie. Come out."

A sob rose in Annie chest. Tears came to her eyes, but she didn't answer.

"Come on, Donny," Jack's daddy called.

Donny turned away and followed Jack and his daddy back down the hill and into the woods.

―――

It was quite dark at eight-thirty when Mike and the boys returned. Mike was clearly embarrassed and distressed that he hadn't found Annie. "It's dark. We got a waning moon. Won't be up 'til near midnight. Even with the flashlight, we can't see any tracks. Trail led up to a big cliff. She couldn't have climbed that. We looked all around it, but no luck. I can come back in the morning."

A dark wave of despair swept through Meg, but she managed to make herself say, "Thank you so much for looking. I'll call my husband. No need to come in the morning. He can be here by then."

There were a few more awkward exchanges, then the Martins left.

Meg turned from the front door as the sound of the Martins' truck faded away. Donny sat at the bottom of the stairs. He looked pale and exhausted and near tears.

"She's hiding," he said. "I bet we were right close to her, calling her, but she's scared or something and wouldn't come out. It's real dark up there, and there's wild animals. What are we going to do, Ma?"

Donny needed her. She struggled to push aside her fears and reassure him. "I'm going to call Daddy. He'll come right away when he hears Annie's lost. He can coax her out of her hiding place."

"But, Ma, Daddy's a long way away. It'll take hours for him to get here. Annie can't stay up in the woods all night. There might be bears. Jonah lives near the woods like we do. He said his daddy chased a bear away from their trash can."

Bears! Meg hadn't thought of that. Panic ran through her like ice water in her veins. Were there really bears up there? Would a bear attack a little girl? Tension from her swirling belly rose up through her neck. Her eyes blurred. Her head felt as if it were gripped in a vice.

"I can take a flashlight and go back by myself," Donny said. "Maybe she was scared of Jack's dad. Maybe she'll come out if it is just me calling her."

"NO!" The mere thought ratcheted Meg's panic up another notch. "I can't have both of you lost up there in the dark." She knew who it was Annie was scared of and it wasn't Jack's dad. She took a few long, slow breaths, but that did nothing to stop her inner trembling. She had to take care of Donny. Still struggling with her terror, she held out her hand to him. "Let's get you cleaned up and tucked in. Then I'll call Daddy."

Annie stayed a long time looking out between the branches. She watched the sky darken. Every so often she saw a light flickering among the trees below. Maybe they were still looking for her and Jack's daddy had a flashlight.

Annie wished she had a flashlight. She thought of all the things Daddy brought when they went camping. Sleeping mats and blankets and pillows. A tent with mosquito netting. Flashlights for each of them. And food.

It was too dark to go home now. Without a flashlight she couldn't find her path.

Finally she crawled back to the cave and lay down by it. The spruce needles weren't soft like her bed. They prickled her bare arms and her neck. Her mosquito bites itched and more mosquitoes hummed around her. She didn't have a pillow.

She sat up and picked up the kittens. Holding them in one hand, she spread the pink towel out, then laid the kittens down on the part of the towel at the very back of the cave. It was almost too dark to see what she was doing. Misty watched the procedure, then lay down by her babies. Annie lay down, too, with her cheek on the other end of the pink towel. She curled her body around the mouth of the cave, her stick near at hand, and drifted back to the elves' magic castle.

Chapter 6

Annie was startled awake by a loud hooting sound. Her eyes flew open to total darkness. Even with her eyes wide open, she couldn't see anything, not anything at all. At first she didn't know where she was. She stirred, and felt prickly spruce needles on her arms. Slowly, realization came. She was under the spruce tree and it was night. Mosquitoes buzzed around her. It was hot and stuffy.

She moved her hand and felt the towel under her cheek. Reached a little further and touched Misty's fur. Misty responded with a soft purr-meow.

Another deep, bone-chilling hoot. Annie jumped. It was close. Right above her. An owl, that's what it was. She and Donny had heard owls hooting in the woods when they were safe at home, tucked in bed. Mama had told them the owls went out hunting for rabbits and mice at night. This owl must be up in the same tree that Annie was lying under.

With a chill, she realized that if owls ate rabbits, they might eat kitties.

Annie groped around for her stick. But what good would a stick do when she couldn't see? Mama had said owls had big eyes and could see at night. But Annie couldn't see anything. If the fox came, she wouldn't be able to see him either. Still she clutched her stick and huddled closer to Misty.

After a while she heard another hoot, but farther off. Maybe the owl had flown away.

Annie lay curled tightly, barely breathing. Every sinew of her body was tensed. She stared into the blackness. Never had she known such darkness. Mama always kept a nightlight in her and Donny's room in case they had to get up in the night and go pee. There was another light in the bathroom.

Thinking of the bathroom made her realize she had to go pee now. There was no nightlight to guide her, no toilet. She remembered how, when they were camping, Mama had taught her to pull down her pants and squat. But she couldn't do that under her tree. The space under her tree was her room. She'd have to go outside the branches.

Slowly she sat up. If she crawled away from her cave, how could she find her way back? She reached around in the darkness and felt the walls of the cave. Maybe if she turned her back on the cave and crawled in a straight line, she could find her way out to the ledge.

The urge to pee became stronger. She mustn't wet her pants. She began to crawl, putting a hand ahead of her to feel where she was going. The spruce needles were prickly under her hands and knees. First a hand, then a knee, then the other hand, the other knee. It felt as if she'd been crawling a long time, when her reaching hand touched the trunk of the tree.

A landmark in the darkness. She crawled close to the trunk, sat up, and leaned against it. She laid her cheek on the rough texture of the bark and felt comforted. This was her tree. It felt like a gentle mama.

But she still had to pee really badly. "I'll be back," she whispered to her tree and began crawling again. At last she saw something. The faintest light, barely a light at all, but a dimness outlining the branches in front of her. Her hand felt branches brushing earth. She pushed through and came out onto the ledge above the cliff.

She stood up, brushed spruce needles off her hands, and gazed around in wonder. She could see! It was all dim, it was night still, but she could make out the black shapes of trees against a star-filled sky. But why could she see, when she couldn't under the tree? She tilted her head back. It must be the stars. She hadn't known that stars could give light, even if it was only a dim light. She could see the shape of the ledge with the woods gathered around it on three sides and the cliff dropping off into darkness close beside her. She stepped away from the edge with a shiver. She had to be careful. If she fell off the cliff, it would really, really hurt and she might not be able to get back to protect Misty and the kittens.

Moving carefully, she walked away from the cliff to the edge of the woods. The urge to pee was almost out of control. It was hard to undo the straps of her overalls, but she finally got them loose and pulled them and her panties down. She peed a lot. She realized she hadn't peed at all since she'd run away. Her pee splattered off the rocky ledge and wet her legs and the bottoms of her overalls. Mama would be mad at her for getting her pants wet.

No. Mama wasn't there. Annie had run away and might never go home again. She might never ever see Mama again. She felt small and alone, the night so dim, the trees around her tall and dark. She needed to get back to her cave and Misty and the kittens. She pulled up her pants and fastened the overall straps.

As she started to walk toward her tree, she stumbled over a loose stone and fell to her hands and knees. One hand slid on the rough stone of the ledge. It hurt a lot. She put her hand to her mouth and tasted blood. Tears welled up. Mama wasn't there to wash it and put iodine and a bandaid on it and kiss it to make it better.

There was no one to take care of her. A wave of desolation swept through her. Still sucking her injured hand, Annie sank down on the ledge, curled on her side. Pointy rocks dug into her hip. She rolled onto her back.

Oh, the stars! She forgot about her hand as she gazed up at the deep arc of the night sky. The stars were so far and yet so near. In the woods around her, they looked like jewels hung in the branches of the trees, like the lights in the leaves of the elves' magic castle.

Yet she knew the stars were far, far away. Daddy had told her that you could fly in an airplane for your whole life and never even get near a star. But if the sky could be far away and still be all around her, maybe the stars could, too. Maybe their light was reaching down and touching her. She lay still, looking up at the stars, imagining that their light was caressing her, comforting her.

A shadow blotted out the stars. The shape of a really big bird. It floated silently above her, wings spread wide. It didn't even flap its wings, just soared over the ledge and cliff, down over the open space below. Annie sat up to watch it. Just before it reached the woods, it folded its wings and dropped swiftly to the ground. Annie heard an anguished squeak. As the bird flapped its wings and lifted into a nearby tree, Annie thought she saw the shape of a tiny body dangling from its claws. Maybe it was a mouse.

She had stopped breathing. Her eyes were pressed wide open in the dim light, her body tense and motionless. The night was still. After a while, from the woods below, Annie heard the same scary hooting sound she'd heard before. That shadow bird must have been the owl. She'd never dreamed an owl would be that big.

Then there was a rustle at the edge of the woods. A snuffling sound. Annie jerked herself around, staring where the sound came from. A dark shape, barely discernible amongst the dim shapes of the undergrowth, moved in a hunching sort of way. It didn't look like a fox shape, but it was big, maybe big enough to eat a kitty. And she was far away from the cave and her stick.

The thought jerked her into action. She spun and crawled as fast as she could to her tree. Complete darkness enfolded her as soon as she went under the branches. She tried to remember where the trunk of the tree was and crawled blindly in that direction. She went what felt like a long way, reaching ahead of herself with her hands. Finally she felt something, but it wasn't the tree trunk. It was a rock and there were stalky things on it. The kittens' grave. She had gone way off to one side.

She felt the earth under her sloping down. She was at the edge of the shelter that was going downhill. She had lost her way.

Panic almost immobilized her. But she had to get back to her cave and her stick in case the snuffly thing came under the tree. She sat up and tried to figure how to find the cave. It was so dark. Then she remembered that the kittens' grave was near the edge where the branches touched the earth and so was the cave. Hoping she was going in the right direction, she started crawling again, hand reaching, knee following, tracing with her lead hand the place where the branches touched the earth. At last she felt the side of the cave, the opening, the towel, Misty's soft fur and the two tiny bodies nestled against her. She felt around some more and found her stick.

The night was silent. No hooting, no snuffling. The spruce needles made a soft cushion, even if they were prickly. Annie lay down, trembling suddenly with weariness and relief. Stick in hand, she curled around the mouth of the cave.

Once Donny was settled, Meg went downstairs to the phone. He had to answer. She needed to hear his voice, to know he was on his way home to her. But when he came, she'd have to tell him what she had done. She hesitated by the phone, her longing colliding with her fear. Her hand shook as she picked up the receiver.

"Number please." The operator's nasal voice. It was so unpleasant the way people talked in New Jersey.

Meg held her breath as she listened to the faraway rings. Four, five …

"Hello." It wasn't Jesse; it was his brother.

"Hello, Walter. This is Meg. Is Jesse there?"

"Yes. Just a minute."

Then Jesse's dear voice. "Meg. I've been wanting to talk with you. I've got great news. I had—"

"You need to come home. Right away. Annie's lost."

"What? Annie's lost?" Jesse's usually calm voice shot up in pitch. "Where? What do you mean, lost? What happened?"

Meg's words poured out in a rush. "She went up in the woods this morning and hasn't come back. Donny went looking for her around noon, but he couldn't find her, and this evening Mr. Martin, Jack's father, and Jack and Donny went to look until after dark, but they didn't find her either. Donny thinks she's hiding and won't come out even when they call her. And now it's dark and she's up there all alone and couldn't find her way home even if she wanted to."

"What happened?" Jesse's voice was hard now. "Why would she be hiding?"

"Jesse, just come home. We need you."

There was silence on the other end of the line. Meg sensed that Jesse was trying to pull himself together. Then he spoke again, sounding more like himself. "Of course I'll come. But remember it's a long drive, and I'll have to find gas, which may be hard at this time of night. Why didn't you call me sooner?"

"I tried, but you didn't answer."

"I've been here since six."

"Jesse, she's up in the woods alone, and there's wild animals. Bears."

"Try to calm yourself, Meg. I'll come as soon as I can." A silence. Meg heard Jesse slowly letting out his breath. "Try not to worry too much. Annie's a resourceful little girl, and probably has found a hiding place that's safe. And when I get home, I'll find her. Is Donny okay?"

"He's here, but he's worried."

"Of course. Take good care of him and of yourself. I'll be there by morning."

Click. He was gone. What if he couldn't find gas? Oh, she should have called sooner. She should have kept calling. But she'd been distracted by the Martins and hoped they'd find Annie and she wouldn't ever have to tell Jesse that Annie was lost and why.

Donny was at the top of the stairs. "I want to talk to Daddy."

"No, you can't. He already hung up. But he's coming home. He's going to start right away, and he'll be here when you wake up in the morning. You get back in bed now."

"I'm hot."

"Yes, it's hot. But there's nothing to be done about that. Get back in bed." Meg heard her voice growing sharp, felt her tension rising.

Clearly Donny felt it, too. He disappeared from the top of the steps.

Meg turned away from the phone and wandered into the kitchen. When she saw the big pot of stew sitting on the stove, she suddenly remembered how hungry she was. She lifted the lid. The stew was still warm and smelled so good that it made Meg feel almost faint. She took a bowl from the cupboard, filled it, and sat down at the dining room table.

Eat slowly, she told herself, but it was hard not to just gobble the stew down. She emptied the bowl in almost no time. It tasted delicious, but her stomach was uneasy when she finished. After all, she'd eaten too fast. And, of course, she was tense.

She'd have to put the stew in the refrigerator, but the big pot wouldn't fit. She set to work ladling the stew into three canning jars. Her hands were shaking again and she slopped some of the precious stew onto the counter. Once the stew was in the jars, she had to move things around in the little refrigerator until she could wedge the three jars in.

She washed the pot. She'd have to return it. Maybe that was a good thing. Maybe Ada would ask her to come in and they'd visit a little. Ada was definitely low class. Meg remembered her poor grammar and the way she'd sat in the big chair with her legs wide apart so you could see the shape of her crotch through her tight jeans.

But she was kind. Really kind. Bringing the stew and understanding as she'd said, "When there's trouble, it's awful hard to think about cooking." And Mike was kind, too, to spend so long looking for Annie. Maybe, Meg thought, she was being too snooty. People could be good and kind even if they weren't well bred. And it had been nice having another woman to chat with.

As she set the clean pot upside down at the edge of the sink, she imagined herself returning the pot, being asked in, what she'd say, what they might talk about.

Then her thoughts returned to Annie, and fear coursed through her again. The outside light by the back door was still on. Meg turned it off and peered out into the darkness. By the dim light of the stars, Meg could see the black shapes of the trees flowing up the hill. Somewhere up there in the dark woods, her beloved little girl was hiding. Jesse said she was resourceful and would find a safe place. Could any place be safe up there in the woods and the night? Was she burrowed under a bush? Were Misty and the remaining kittens with her? And what, oh what, had she done with the dead ones?

Nauseous guilt turned in her stomach. If only she'd thought things through before she'd acted. She'd *known* how attached Annie was to those kittens. She never should have drowned them. If only she hadn't, then Annie would be safe upstairs in her bed.

But there were too many, and no money to feed her children, much less six cats. And, of course, she'd never imagined that Annie would witness the drowning.

Like a sudden whirlwind inside her, guilt twisted to rage. It was Jesse's fault. A college professor who couldn't keep a job.

She turned away from the door and paced the small kitchen.

She remembered their courtship, how deeply she had fallen in love with him. There was such a clarity about him, a level of integrity that she'd never encountered before. He cared for all people no matter what their race or background. When he gave her his love, she'd known he would be true to her, that he would never lie to her, that she could trust him.

Even her parents had approved of him. It was true that he was a lot older than Meg, but he was handsome and fit and gracious, a professor in a small college in western Massachusetts. Meg had imagined that she and Jesse would settle down there in the lovely college town surrounded by intelligent, educated people.

No one, least of all Meg, could have guessed that Jesse's impeccable integrity would be their downfall.

Why couldn't he play along, overlook the dishonesty, the rotten politics, the racial prejudice. Such things were part of every institution, weren't they? But he couldn't. He had to speak up. Then his contract wasn't renewed. Twice this had happened. Two good positions lost. Each time they had come back to live with his mother and sister. And now he'd been out of work for a year, except for his stint on the road crew.

Her father had known how to play along, and had worked his way up to a substantial salary as dean at a big university. Her mother, who'd brought her own considerable wealth to the marriage, played along too. Meg was glad her parents hadn't lived to see her descend to her present miserable situation.

Even as she raged, Meg knew their playing along had tainted them in a way Jesse would never be tainted. She remembered their faces, the masks of charm and propriety. In contrast, Meg saw Jesse's clear eyes, his open face. Something wanted to soften inside her, but she turned fiercely away from it.

He had put his precious integrity ahead of supporting his family. Left her in this god-forsaken factory borough that wasn't even big enough to be called a town, alone with two little kids and no money.

She found she was leaning against the sink, staring out into the dark woods. She shuddered. It was like an evil presence brooding over her, swallowing her child. She turned back to the door and flipped the light on again. Vain hope it could guide Annie home.

Damn Jesse. If he had been here, if he had sent her money, none of this would have happened.

She paced into the living room. Her fists were clenched. She wanted to smash something.

A fragment of the blue vase that had eluded her earlier cleanup crunched under her foot. A wave of grief rose up in her—for the lost vase and all that it represented. She unclenched her fists. No, she didn't want to smash anything. Enough had been lost.

She went to the pantry for the dustpan and brush, swept up the fragments, and poured them into the kitchen wastebasket. She couldn't face the trash can out back again.

What could she do with herself? How could she endure this night?

She wandered back into the living room and dropped down into the big chair. The *Ladies' Home Journal* was on the table beside her. Rage stormed up in her again. What kind of life was she living that she would be reading such pulp? She who had graduated with honors from Vassar. She stood up and threw the magazine across the room. It hit the bookcase and slid down into a crumpled pile on the floor.

She needed to calm down, she told herself. Jesse said to calm down. Maybe she should check on Donny. What if he'd gone out into the night to look for Annie after all? She knew he could climb out the bedroom window and down the big tree that grew there close to the house. He'd done it before. Panic swept through her. She hurried up the stairs.

It was much hotter up there. Quietly, she moved to the open door of the children's room. Donny was in his bed and seemed to be sleeping.

Meg let out a long sigh. Maybe she should try to rest, too. Under all the tension, she knew she was exhausted. But not up here. It was too hot.

She went back downstairs and lay down on the couch.

Annie dreamed. The same bad dream. The witch's goblins were chasing her through the dark woods again. Annie ran, gasping, screaming for her mama. But Mama was the witch. She came through the trees, tall and terrible, her face contorted in a mean smile that showed her yellow, pointed teeth. With her piercing claws, she grabbed Annie by her shoulders. Annie was tiny, like the tiny body of the mouse in the owl's claws. The witch lifted her high in the air. Annie looked down and saw the rain barrel beneath her. Holding Annie in one claw, the witch lifted the cover of the rain barrel. Annie screamed, "No! No! Don't drown me," but the only sound that came out of her was the squeak of a mouse. The witch laughed a horrible laugh. Then her arm swung down and plunged Annie into black, frigid water.

Annie woke choking and sobbing. In her dream the water had been icy cold, but she was sweating, shaking all over. "No, Mama," she sobbed. Gradually she remembered where she was. She reached out her hand and touched Misty's warm, furry body. Misty responded with a soft, inquiring meow, then came to her and began licking the tears on Annie's cheeks with her small, rough tongue. Annie gathered Misty close to her heart, laid her cheek against Misty's soft fur, and breathed in Misty's special smell. Gradually her sobs quieted.

"I had the bad dream again," she whispered to her cat. "Only this time it was even badder, because Mama was drowning me in the rain barrel like she did Dapple and Tiger and Smokey."

She lay holding Misty close, grieving anew for her lost kittens.

After a while, Misty slipped away. Annie rolled over onto her back. It wasn't totally dark anymore, she realized. There were tiny bits of light showing between the branches above her.

Was it morning? Curious, she sat up, then stood. There was barely enough light, but she could just make out the shape of the tree trunk. She went to it and leaned against it.

Then, still curious about the light, she dropped to her hands and knees and crawled out from under the tree and onto the ledge. She got to her feet and looked around. The light was much brighter there than under the tree. But it wasn't morning. A half moon hung over the valley below. In its light, Annie could see her shadow stretching out long across the ledge.

"I didn't know the moon made shadows," she said aloud. Moon shadows!

She waved her arms, watching her shadow move. Then she walked around looking at other moon shadows—the shadow of a jutting rock, the shadows of the trees at the back of the ledge flowing into the darkness of the deep woods, even the thin shadows of tall grasses growing at the edge of the cliff.

Then another shadow. Misty scampered toward her, her lively shadow running beside her.

For a short while, Annie forgot her grief and fear in the wonder of moon shadows. She and Misty walked all around the ledge looking at them.

Annie was bent down to see how small a rock could make a shadow, when suddenly another shadow fell over her—huge with wide-spread wings. She had just realized it was the owl shadow, when she saw the wings fold. A rush of air. The folded-wing shadow dived toward Misty.

"NO!" Annie screamed and lunged to shield her cat. A heavy blow from above knocked her forward onto her face. At the same moment she felt a searing pain across her shoulder and caught a quick glimpse of Misty streaking into the shelter of the tree.

Then the owl shadow was gone.

Annie hurt so much. The blow and the fall had knocked the breath out of her. The burning pain in her shoulder hurt worse than anything that had ever happened to her. She lay sprawled on the ledge, too stunned to move or cry.

Far below, she heard the hooting of the owl.

Meg woke and found herself on the couch. Moonlight was coming in the east window, making a luminous path across the living room rug.

She sat up, feeling cramped and sticky. Her dress was twisted around her, wrinkled. She looked at the moonlight on the rug. Mike had said the moon wouldn't be up until after midnight. What time was it? She looked at her watch. Five after two. She'd been asleep.

How could she just sleep when Annie was lost? But what use was it for her to stay awake? It didn't matter what she did. Everything she did was wrong.

She stood and yanked her dress straight, walked to the east window and looked down on the road, the valley below, the half-moon hanging low in the sky. The living room was the only room in the house with three windows. All the windows were open, but no air moved in the stifling night.

Meg paced to the west window. Like the kitchen window, it looked out into the woods. Moonlight penetrated only a little way into the trees. Beyond, the woods were a mass of darkness. But maybe the moon was bright enough that Annie could find her way home. Maybe she'd slipped in quietly while Meg was asleep. Unable to stifle the hope in her heart, Meg climbed the stairs and peered into the children's room. Donny had kicked off his sheet and shed his pajama top. He lay sprawled on his back, snoring softly. Annie's bed was empty.

Meg turned away. "Déjà vu, déjà vu," she muttered to herself as she went back down the stairs. "Fall asleep on the couch, imagine Annie has come in while you sleep, climb the stairs to look. She isn't there. You already did that this afternoon. You're going nuts."

Meg went back to the living room couch and hunched there, her knees drawn up to her chest.

Where, oh where, was Annie? What was happening to her?

Jesse said he would find her. Was he really sure, or was he just trying to calm her down? And what would he find? Terrifying images rose behind Meg's eyes. A broken heap at the base of a cliff. A mangled child half eaten by a wild animal. Meg remembered reading a newspaper article about a camper in Colorado who was hauled out of his tent by a bear that had clamped down on his head. What if a bear found Annie under a bush and pulled her out by her head, tearing her beautiful little face, crushing her lively, poetic brain? She'd be a scarred imbecile for the rest of her life. And it would be all Meg's fault.

She wasn't fit to be a mother.

She remembered the hardness in Jesse's voice when he asked what happened. She certainly couldn't tell him on the phone with who-knows-who listening on the party line. How could she tell him anyway?

She knew that, although he was devoted to both children, Annie was his special love. If anything bad happened to Annie, he would never forgive Meg. He would stop loving her. Maybe he would leave and take the children away. Probably he'd give them to Nellie to bring up.

But they were *her* children. She loved them. No one else, especially Nellie, could love them the way Meg did, understand them the way she did. Meg couldn't bear to think of them being brought up in Nellie's sanctified Christianity, having all their natural impulses repressed.

Oh, what had she done? She'd destroyed everything.

If Jesse stopped loving her, if he took the children away from her, how could she go on?

It was her rages, her terrible rages. As if she had an evil demon inside her that she couldn't control. She'd always had a quick temper, yes, but it hadn't always been as bad as it was now. Maybe she had a degenerative mental illness.

Maybe it would be better if Jesse left and took the children away. Then she couldn't harm them again.

An image of the bruise on Annie's cheek assailed her. It had still been there two days after Meg struck her. It must have still been hurting when Annie ran away that morning—yesterday morning now.

Would this night never end?

The moon rose slowly up from the valley and hung directly over the rocky ledge. Annie moved. She stretched out her hand and touched a small, sharp rock. She turned her head and saw the moonlight spilling around her. Slowly, she pulled herself up onto her hands and knees and crawled toward the shelter of her tree. As she ducked underneath, the low hanging branches brushed her shoulder. It hurt so much she cried out. Leaning on one hand, she reached up with the other hand to touch the place of pain. It was sticky and wet. She brought her hand back to her face and smelled blood.

The owl scratched me, she realized. She shuddered at the memory of the owl shadow diving for Misty, the sudden blow from above. She imagined the owl's claws like the witch's claws. For a moment, all was confusion. The owl, the dream, the claws, the terror.

She caught her breath and remembered where she was. She was in the shelter of her tree. She wasn't tiny like she'd been in her dream, like the mouse the owl had caught. She was too big for the owl to carry away. And Misty was safe. Annie had seen her dash under the tree. The owl couldn't get her there.

She *was* safe, wasn't she? Annie had to know. As fast as she could, she crawled toward the cave. The moonlight coming through the spaces between the branches gave enough light for her to find it. Her stick lay across the opening. It was dark inside the cave. She reached inside. She felt nothing but the texture of the pink towel. Her heart stopped. "Misty?" she whispered.

She heard a slight movement. Then her hand touched Misty's soft fur. A sobbing sigh shook her. "Oh, Misty," she whispered. "You're safe. Did you know the owl almost got you? He got me instead, but I was too big for him to carry away. Oh, I'm so glad he didn't get you."

Annie lay down again, curled around the mouth of the cave. She couldn't lie on the side that the owl had scratched. Everything in her body hurt. For a while she dozed and imagined the magic elves coming to take care of her and Misty and the kittens.

A snuffling sound. Close by. Right above her. Annie spun to sitting. Something was moving the branches that touched the top of the cave. In a flash, Annie was on her feet, her stick in her hand. She swept the stick over the top of the cave, screaming, "Get away. Get away." Her stick hit something solid with a thump. She heard a snarling growl and a scrabbling noise in the bushes. Parting the boughs of the spruce, she saw the same animal she'd seen earlier in the undergrowth across the ledge. The same hunching movement. But it was running away. She'd scared it off.

Annie sat down again, trembling. For a brief moment, she felt elation. She'd scared the snuffler away. But now her shoulder hurt. Her sudden movement had torn open the owl scratch and it was bleeding again.

Misty came to sit in her lap. Annie stroked her soft fur. She was Annie's best friend, but the owl had almost gotten her.

Annie began crying, overwhelmed by despair. "I don't know what to do, Misty," she sobbed. "We can't stay here. There's no food or water. And it isn't safe. There's the owl and the fox and the snuffly animal. They all want to eat you. But we can't go home. I'm scared of Mama. I'm afraid she will kill Dusty and Buttercup like she did the others. I'm afraid she'll hit me so hard, and yell at me and call me wicked … Donny said she'd kill me if I didn't go home. And I didn't go home all this time, even all night. And I tore her special basket.

"But we can't stay here. There's no magic elves. I just made them up. No one will come and take care of us. Oh, Misty, what shall we do? I don't know what to do. There's no safe place."

Her sobs overcame her then. Still holding Misty close in her arms, she curled down into the spruce needles and wept until she was too weary to cry anymore. She lay clutching her stick, afraid to sleep; and since she'd told Misty the elves were made up, not real, she couldn't go back to their magic castle.

Chapter 7

Light sifted down between the branches of the spruce tree. Annie opened her eyes. The light around her was morning light, not moonlight. In spite of her determination to stay awake, she had slept again.

She rolled over quickly, then cried out in pain. The owl scratch really hurt. But she had to know if Misty and the kittens were safe. She pushed herself up to sitting and looked into the cave. They were inside, sleeping curled up together. Annie touched Misty's head. Misty opened her wide green eyes and greeted Annie with her dear purr-meow.

There was a brown patch of dried blood where Annie had been lying. She felt awful. Her mouth was dry, her belly was shriveled with hunger and fear, and her eyes burned from so much weeping. Her face and arms were covered with mosquito bites that itched and stung. Worst of all was the throbbing pain in her shoulder. She tried to turn her head to see the scratch, but it was too close to her neck. She put her hand up to touch it, tracing it with her finger. It started partway down her back and came up over her shoulder. Her shirt was torn and a flap of cloth was caught in sticky blood. Spruce needles were stuck in it, too.

Touching the scratch made it hurt worse. It felt hot. She knew it should be washed and have iodine put on it. Even though the iodine stung, it was important so the scratch wouldn't get infected. Maybe the owl's claws had germs that were growing in her scratch right now. Fear coursed through her, leaving her trembling. Maybe the scratch would make her sick and then she couldn't protect the kittens anymore.

She put her sticky fingers in her mouth and moaned. Misty came and sat in Annie's lap, working her paws gently into Annie's thighs. Just the sound of her purr made Annie feel better.

Annie took a deep breath and sat up straighter. She had to go back down the hill to the house. Misty and the kittens weren't safe here. Annie had meant to stay awake to protect them in case the snuffly animal came back, but she had fallen asleep. She couldn't stay awake all the time.

She had to go back. But she'd have to hide the kittens from Mama. Maybe she could hide in the thicket and watch the house, then slip in when Mama wasn't watching and hide the kittens under her bed. But Mama would see her before long, and be mad and hit Annie again and shake her. Maybe Annie would just have to bear that so the kittens would be safe.

Mama was usually gentle after she was mad. Then maybe she'd take care of the owl scratch so Annie wouldn't get sick from it. Maybe Annie could tell her she was sorry about the basket and beg Mama not to hurt Dusty and Buttercup. Maybe she could get Mama to promise she wouldn't.

But what if Mama wouldn't promise? What if she found the kittens under the bed?

Annie relived seeing her mama push Dapple and Tiger and Smokey under the water and throw them in the trash can. Fear poured through her in an icy wave. She saw her mama huge with rage.

She couldn't go back.

But she had to. She had to be brave even if Mama was mad.

She scrambled to her feet. Her head spun. For a moment it seemed as if the tree and the whole hillside tipped. Her stomach turned and her eyes went dark. She barely felt herself crumple down into the spruce needles.

⋅§ ⁊⋅

Meg woke to the low hum of a motor and the sound of wheels crunching on the gravel driveway. Morning light flowed in through the east window. She rolled over, came to her feet and ran to the window. There was Jesse's black Ford in the driveway and Jesse just getting out of the driver's seat. He straightened stiffly, then reached his arms over his head and stretched, his strong, lean form outlined against the morning sky.

Meg's heart ached with love. She ran, opened the front door, and met him on the porch. His arms around her, his cheek against hers. For that moment, all that mattered was that he had come and she was safe in his arms.

He released her and held her back from him, his hands on her shoulders. Gently, he caressed her cheek. He had dark shadows under his eyes and his brow was furrowed.

"Still gone?" he asked.

Meg nodded.

"Let's go in." He led her through the door and closed it behind them.

Donny appeared at the top of the stairs. "Dad!" he yelled and dashed down the stairs. Meg stepped aside as he flung himself at his father. Jesse picked him up and held him close.

Donny looked into his father's face. "Dad, Annie's lost. Can you find her?"

Jesse set Donny down. "That's what I'm here for. And I need you to help me." He ruffled Donny's dark curls. "First I need to talk with Mama for a few minutes. You go on upstairs and get dressed. Then we'll go."

"Okay, Dad." Donny ran back up the stairs.

Jesse took Meg's hand and led her into the living room. He drew her down to sit beside him on the couch and took both her hands in his.

"Tell me what happened. Why has Annie run away?"

The euphoria of his coming home drained out of Meg. She burned with shame and at the same time shivered with fear. She turned her head away, unable to look into his true-blue eyes.

I can't tell him, she thought desperately. I'll lie. I'll tell him the kittens just died, like I was planning to tell the children. But he'll know. Annie will tell him. He'll never forgive me if I lie. I promised to always tell him the truth.

She twisted, turning her head to the other side.

"What is it, Meg?" He was there holding her hands, waiting, patient as he always was with her.

Her stomach heaved. Maybe she was going to throw up. A wave rose up in her throat, and sank back. She coughed, twisted again.

Still unable to look at him, she finally stammered, "I … I did a … terrible thing."

"What did you do?"

"I drowned three of the kittens … in the rain barrel … and I think Annie saw me. I thought she was up on the hill with Donny—"

"You WHAT?" he interrupted her. "You drowned her kittens?"

"Not all of them."

"You drowned three of her kittens and she saw you do it?"

His voice was terrible. She'd never heard him so angry. He let go of her hands, strode across the room to the window, and stood with his back turned toward her. His shoulders were hunched, his fists clenched.

In the long silence that followed, Meg sat frozen on the couch, biting her lower lip, barely breathing.

At last Jesse turned. His voice was quieter, but she could still hear the anger. "How could you? I've never heard Annie so happy as she was on her birthday, telling me each kitten's name and what it looked like. You just snuffed out her happiness. Why?"

Meg surged to standing. "Because …" Her voice rose. "You didn't send me any money. We can't live on nothing. There was no cat food left. Misty was eating a lot to feed five kittens. We were out of people food, too. Nothing for the children and only twenty-seven dollars left. The mail came, and there was no check from you. You said you would send me money, but nothing." She could see the pain in his face, but couldn't stop. "It's your fault. You can't keep a job to support your family. If I have to choose between feeding my children and feeding a bunch of cats, I choose my children."

Jesse put his hand out. "I have a job. I tried to tell you last night. I got the job at Boston University."

"Lovely. And how long will you keep that one? Until you put your foot in your mouth again, and again your contract isn't renewed?"

Jesse stepped back as if she'd struck him. He took in a quick breath as if to speak, then turned his head away.

Meg's rage drained out of her, and tears rose. "I'm sorry, Jesse. I shouldn't have said that. I'm just so tired and so worried."

Jesse let out a long sigh. His shoulders softened and his fists unclenched.

"I'm worried, too, all night driving here." He came to her and took her in his arms again. "We need to talk about all this later. Now I need to find Annie and bring her home. I need a little more information. You think Annie saw you?"

Meg rested her aching head against his shoulder. "She must have. I thought she was up on the hill with Donny, but Donny told me she had come back. I went up in my room after … I was already regretting what I'd done. She must have crept in while I was there with the door shut and taken the other two kittens. When I went to look, the basket was gone. And the dead ones I had thrown in the trash can were gone, too. Donny saw her up in the woods with the basket, but when I sent him back to get her, he couldn't find her. He found the basket. It had gotten torn. Annie will be scared I'll punish her for tearing the basket."

"To say nothing of how frightened she must be of you, after seeing you kill her kittens. Oh, Meg. There's much repairing that will need to be done. But first I must find her."

Donny came thundering down the stairs and into the living room. "I'm ready, Dad."

"Just a minute more."

Jesse turned back to Meg. "She's been up there since yesterday morning with no food or water?"

"I don't think she took anything."

"Fix her some food. I'll get my day pack and canteen." He strode through the house and out to the shed in back and returned with his pack.

Meg met him in the kitchen. "There's almost no food in the house. I was going to go to the store yesterday, but didn't want to leave in case Annie came home. Jack's mom brought us some stew yesterday evening. That's all we have."

"Heat some up and put it in a thermos bottle."

"Just bring her home. We can feed her here."

"She may not be ready to come home right away. I may need to stay with her a while, if she is as frightened as I am guessing she is"

Meg cringed. "But how will I know if you've found her?"

"Donny will come with me. When I find her, he'll come and tell you. Okay, Donny?"

"Okay." Donny was standing very straight, ready to do his part. "I think I know where she is."

Meg grabbed Donny by the shoulders. "You do?"

"I think so. But she's hiding, and wouldn't come out when I called her. I'll show Daddy."

"Good," Jesse said, his voice full of relief. "I'll follow your lead."

Meg set to work heating some stew, rinsing and filling the canteen. Her heart was pounding. Donny knew where Annie was. Maybe they really could find her. Then she suddenly realized what Jesse had told her. She turned to him where he stood beside her in the kitchen. "You got the job?"

"I signed the contract yesterday afternoon. I was going to call you, but you called first, and then all I could think of was Annie. Yes, I did get the job. I think it is going to work this time. I want to tell you all about it later. How's that stew coming?"

"It's ready." Meg poured it out of the pan into the thermos bottle, tucked a spoon and cup into Jesse's pack. All the while her mind was reeling.

"You got the job. That's wonderful, Jesse. I'm so glad."

He came and hugged her. "We're going to be okay now. As soon as I find Annie."

A few minutes later, Meg watched Jesse and Donny walk up the path into the woods. A confusion of conflicting emotions swirled in her. Excitement about Jesse's new job. Boston. There was culture in Boston. She imagined concerts, lectures, plays. Maybe now they could afford music lessons for the children. Maybe Annie would like dance lessons.

Mixed in with the excitement was a new level of anguish. What would Jesse find? Would Annie be okay, or somehow damaged by her night in the woods? And surely her relationship with Meg was damaged. Could it ever be mended? Would Annie ever forgive her, ever trust her again?

Annie lay curled up with her eyes closed. Daddy was singing to her, one of her favorite songs. She thought she was in bed and Daddy was downstairs, playing the piano and singing her to sleep the way he did when he was home. Only there was no piano, just his sweet, clear voice singing, "I'll be loving you, always."

She stirred. Her shoulder hurt. Her eyes opened. Sunlight filtered down through the branches of the spruce tree. She wasn't in bed at home, she was under the tree and she hurt all over. But still she could hear Daddy singing, "With a love that's true, always."

Slowly, stiffly she sat up. Daddy? Was she making it up, like the elves and their magic castle? But his voice sounded real and near.

"When the things you've planned
Need a helping hand
I will understand …"

Daddy! Maybe it really was Daddy and he had come to find her. As fast as she could, she crawled toward the sound of his voice, past the trunk of the tree, toward the place where the spruce branches touched the ledge. Her heart was pounding. With a tentative hand, she pushed a branch aside and peered through.

It *was* Daddy. He sat only a few feet away from her, cross-legged, the way he always sat on the ground, his day pack beside him. The morning sun lit up his face. He was real!

He had seen her. He smiled at her with the special smile he had only for her and held out his arms, still singing, "Always, always."

She scrambled to her feet to run to him, but her head spun again and she stumbled. He caught her and gathered her into his lap, folded her in his arms.

"Annie," he said softly, "I'm so glad to see you."

"Daddy." She could hardly believe he was really there. But his arms felt real around her. She could smell his special smell. The owl scratch hurt when he hugged her, but she didn't care. He was talking to her now in his real voice.

"How are you, sweetheart?"

The ache in her heart felt as if it would break her into pieces. "I'm really sad."

"Tell me."

"Mama killed my kittens and threw them in the trash can. They were all cold and wet and Misty wouldn't lick them. She just took them off the towel and scratched spruce needles over them. They got all stiff and ants got on them. So I buried them good in the ground and put a rock over their grave, and flowers. But now they'll never grow up, and I'll never know what color their eyes were going to be." Sobs overcame her then. She turned her face into her daddy's shoulder and wept, her whole body aching and shaking with her grief.

He held her, gently stroking her hair. When at last she quieted he said, "Oh, Annie, I'm so sorry. Mama is sorry, too. She told me."

"She shouldn't have done that. They were *my* kittens. Misty gave them to me for my birthday. And she just killed them."

"You're right. She shouldn't have. What about the other two kittens? What were their names?"

"Dusty and Buttercup. I brought them up here and hid them in my cave so Mama wouldn't kill them, too. But there's a fox and an owl and a snuffly animal, and they all want to eat Misty and the kittens. The owl almost got Misty, but I got in the way and he scratched me."

"I can see. It looks like a bad scratch. And you have a bump on your head, too." He stroked her hair and she felt the sore place on the back of her head where the bump was. "How did that happen?"

"I was pulling a stick out of the tree. At first it wouldn't come and then it came all at once and I fell on my back." Annie sat up straight in Daddy's lap. "I needed a big stick in case the fox came."

Her throat was itchy and she coughed.

"Sounds like you're kind of dry. Would you like some water? I brought you some."

Water! "Yes, please."

Daddy pulled his day pack over beside him and brought out a canteen. He unscrewed the top and handed it to her. The water was cool in her mouth, cool in her throat. She could feel it running all the way down into her tummy.

"Easy," Daddy said, tipping the canteen away from her mouth. "A little at a time. There's plenty."

She caught her breath and reached for the canteen again. Water had never tasted so good.

"I bet you're hungry, too. Jack's mama brought some stew over to our house last night. I have some here in my pack."

At the thought of food, Annie's jaws tingled and saliva filled her mouth. She watched as Daddy pulled a thermos and cup and spoon out of his pack. When he poured the stew into the cup, the smell was so delicious it made her dizzy.

She ate.

"Not too fast," Daddy cautioned her. "Let your tummy get used to having food again after such a long time."

She slowed down only a little. It tasted so good. She began to feel better all over. When she had finished eating, Daddy took her back into his lap. She snuggled against him, feeling happiness spread through her in spite of her sadness about the kittens.

"Why did you stay away so long?" Daddy asked.

"I'm scared Mama will kill the other kittens. And she'll be really mad at me, because I tore her special basket, and didn't come home when she rang the bell, and I peed on my overalls."

Daddy was silent, just holding her close. After a while, he said, "You've had lots of adventures up here in the woods. I want to know about the fox and the owl and that other creature, the snuffly one. Would you tell me your story, like a story in a book? But this would be a true story, not a made-up one. About what really happened to you. Begin at the beginning and tell me all your adventures."

Annie sighed and settled closer in his arms. She told him the whole story beginning with seeing Mama drowning the kittens—the flight to the cave, the torn basket, the fox and the stick, the kittens' grave, the night. Starlight and moon shadows. The owl catching the mouse and diving for Misty. The snuffly animal.

When she finished her story, she uncurled from Daddy's arms and looked into his face. "I thought if I brought my kittens to the cave, we'd be safe. But it isn't safe here. There's too many wild animals and I can't stay awake all the time to protect the kittens. After I chased away the snuffly animal, I fell asleep, even though I tried to watch, and when I woke up, I knew it wasn't safe and I had to go home. But when I got up, my head was dizzy and I fell down. Then you came."

Daddy held her a little tighter. "You're safe now. I'm going to take care of you and help you take care of your kittens." He gently set her off his lap onto her feet and stood. "We need to go home. Mama is worried and we need to take care of that owl scratch."

Annie felt a fear shiver go through her. "But what if Mama …"

"Mama won't hurt your kittens. She's really sorry about the other ones."

"But she'll be really mad at me and hit me."

"No." Daddy's voice was stern. "She will not hit you. I'll make sure of that."

"But then you'll go away." As soon as she said that, Annie wished she hadn't because Daddy's face changed. He looked sad and mad both. She shrank away from him.

He squatted down in front of her and put his hands on her waist. "Annie, I'm sorry I've been away so long. But I have a job now. We'll all move up to Boston and find a nice house to live in. I'll still need to go to work in the daytime, but I'll be home every night before supper and every morning when you wake up. I'm not going to leave you again. Do you understand?"

His face was level with hers. She looked into his eyes. He was really sad.

"I understand," she said.

"Good." He stood up again. "Now let's find your kittens and go home. Where are they?"

"They're in my cave. It's under the tree. But I haven't been watching it." Suddenly Annie was afraid. "I hope the snuffly animal didn't come back. I better go look."

"May I come, too?"

"You can, but you mustn't tell Donny where it is. It's *my* cave, and if he knew about it, then he'd want to be the boss of it."

"I won't tell Donny."

"You have to scrunch down." Annie got on her hands and knees to show him.

Daddy got on his hands and knees, too. Annie led him under the tree and over to the cave. Misty was nursing her kittens. She looked up and greeted Annie with a soft meow.

"This is a wonderful cave," Daddy said, "all hidden under the tree."

"And here is where I buried Smokey and Dapple and Tiger." Annie couldn't help the little quiver in her voice when she said their names. She led him over to the grave. The flowers had already wilted.

Daddy touched the stone. "You found a pretty stone with mica in it." He turned around, back toward the cave. "Show me where you chased the snuffly animal away."

"Up here." Annie stood up and touched the top of the cave. "He was snuffling in the branches, right here."

Daddy couldn't stand up straight under the tree, but he got up and bent over to look under the branches. "See here," he said. "There's some tracks. See these prints in the dust, like a long narrow hand?"

Annie looked. Sure enough, there were prints in the dust on the top of the cave.

"Those are raccoon tracks. You're right. He was dangerous. He would have been glad to eat the kittens and Misty, too. It's good you scared him away." He got back down on his hands and knees. "Bring your kittens now. How will you carry them?"

"I'll make a pocket in the towel, like this." She sat down in the cave and gently lifted the kittens into her lap. They seemed used to her touch and didn't squeal at all. Then she folded the towel into a pocket and put the kittens into it. Misty watched closely.

"And how will you get down the cliff?"

"Here." Annie showed him the beginning of her tunnel beside the cliff.

Daddy peered down it. "I can't go that way very easily. I'll climb down the cliff and meet you at the bottom. Okay?"

"Okay." Annie watched him crawl out from under the tree. She paused a moment to look at the cave, the grave with the wilted flowers, and the circular space under the branches. She got a funny feeling inside. It had been her shelter, but she'd been so sad and scared there. She wanted to go rest against the tree trunk one last time, but Daddy would be waiting.

She turned and backed out from under the branches down into her tunnel, with Misty following her. She came out at the bottom just in time to see Daddy climb down the cliff. He did it easily and didn't look scared at all even though it was so high and steep.

Daddy came to her and squatted down in front of her again so he could look into her face. "Annie, I'm proud of you. You have been brave and resourceful."

"What does sourceful mean?"

"Resourceful. It means you figured out lots of ways to protect your kittens, how to use the trowel to get the stick out of the tree, and the way you dived over Misty to protect her from the owl. That was very brave."

"But if the owl had gotten Misty I would never stop crying. She's my best friend."

"And you are a best friend to her. Shall we go down now?"

He took her hand, but her legs were all wobbly, and she stumbled. He bent and picked her up. "How about you carry the kittens, and I'll carry you."

He held her close in his strong arms, being careful not to squeeze her owl scratch. She rested her head on his shoulder. As they started down the hill, with Misty running beside them, he sang again.

"Days may not be fair, always.

That's when I'll be there, always.

Not for just an hour, not for just a day, not for just a year,

But always."

Chapter 8

Daddy was able to just walk down the hill; he didn't have to duck under the bushes the way Annie had. There was a clear path now, with branches pushed aside. Maybe Jack's daddy had done it the night before. Annie didn't like the path being so wide. It made her cave less secret.

The farther down they went, the more scared Annie felt. Even with Daddy holding her, she was scared to see her mama, scared of what Mama would do. And she never wanted Mama to touch her kittens again.

They reached the fort. Annie lifted her head from his shoulder. "Wait, Daddy."

Daddy stopped walking. "What is it?"

"I don't want to go home."

"Why not?"

Annie couldn't answer. Fear clotted her throat.

Daddy smoothed her back with his hand. "What is it? Are you scared?"

"Uh huh."

"Of Mama?"

She pushed her face into his shoulder and nodded.

Daddy sat down on the ground in front of the fort and shifted her into his lap.

The kittens stirred in their pocket in the towel. Annie cradled the towel in the curve of her arm and looked down at the tiny creatures she had struggled so hard to keep safe. With the tip of her finger, she stroked Dusty's little gray head and Buttercup's yellow one. Dusty pushed his head back against Annie's finger. It was the first time any of the kittens had responded to Annie's touch. Love and joy burst like a blossom in her heart.

"Look, Daddy. Dusty's nudging me. He likes me to touch him."

Daddy looked down at her. "There's your smile!" he said. He was smiling, too. "It looks like he does like you to touch him."

Annie stroked the kittens' heads again and leaned back against Daddy's shoulder. He sat quietly with her for a little while. Then he said, "We do need to go home, Annie. We need to clean up that owl scratch and get the kittens settled in a safe place so Misty can take care of them."

Misty had followed them down the hill and was sitting close to Annie and Daddy.

Annie didn't say anything.

Daddy continued. "I've told you how brave you have been to protect the kittens from all those wild animals. Now you need to be brave again and go home to your mama. We're a family and we all need to live together and get along and take care of each other. I'm sorry you are scared of Mama and I understand why. But I'll be with you and help you. Mama's very sorry she killed your kittens. She was worried she didn't have enough food for the kittens and you and Donny."

"But Misty was feeding the kittens."

"But she'll only feed them for a little while. Then they'll need solid food like Misty."

"I would give them some of my food."

"I'm sure you would. But there's no need. I've brought Mama some money and we can have all the food we want now." He shifted Annie in his lap. "Shall we go?"

Annie didn't want to go. She didn't want to see Mama ever again. She just wanted to sit there in the woods in Daddy's lap. But he had asked her to be brave.

"Okay," she whispered.

"Atta girl." He stood and picked her up again and began walking on down the hill.

They came out of the woods into the back yard. There was the rain barrel and the trash can. There was Mama at the back door. Annie turned her face into Daddy's shoulder. She heard the screen door open and shut, heard Daddy's footsteps change as he walked into the kitchen. It smelled like the stew Daddy had brought her. Annie was hungry again and wanted more, but she kept her face hidden against Daddy's shoulder.

She heard Mama talking. "Thank God! Thank God you found her." Then she heard Mama crying. Annie turned her head a little and peeked at Mama. Mama looked bad. She had purple smudges under her eyes and her hair was all messed up. And she looked really sad—and scared. How could Mama be scared? But she was. Annie could see the scared look in her eyes.

Annie's feelings were all mixed up. She didn't want Mama to be sad and cry. Maybe Mama loved Annie and was sad and worried because Annie had been gone all night. Annie wanted Mama to love her. But she was also mad at Mama for killing her kittens. She hated Mama. She was glad Mama was crying. She wanted to kick her mama and hit her. She wanted Mama to hold her, and she never wanted Mama to touch her again. And even though Mama was crying and looking sad and as if she would be gentle, Annie was scared of her.

Mama had come up to Daddy, holding out her arms. "Give her to me." She touched Annie.

Annie shrank away from her hand, shielded the kittens with her body, and pressed her face deeper into Daddy's shoulder.

She felt Mama step back.

Daddy held her closer. "Give her a little time," he said.

Mama was crying more. "What happened to her? She's got blood all over her."

"She had an incident with an owl," Daddy said.

"An owl! Please give her to me. Her shoulder's all torn up and she's covered with mosquito bites. I need to take care of her."

Daddy was still holding her close. "I think it's best that I take care of her now." Annie kept her face pressed against him. She heard Mama draw in her breath. The room was still for a moment. Then Daddy continued talking to Mama. "Why don't you go to the store and get us some food. It's almost eight; the store will be open soon. Annie's had some stew, but she'll need something more. And I could use a good breakfast. There's money in my wallet. The car key and wallet are on the bookcase. Will you go with her, Donny, and help her?"

"Okay."

Donny. Annie peeked again. He was standing near Mama looking up at Annie with round eyes. When he saw her peeking at him, he came to her and touched her leg. "I'm real glad you're home," he said.

Annie didn't know how to respond, but it felt warm and good that Donny cared about her.

Daddy moved. "You two go along now. I'll get Annie settled."

He took her upstairs. They laid the kittens on Annie's bed, and Misty, who had followed, jumped up and started licking them. Daddy helped Annie out of her clothes, gave her a warm bath, and put iodine on her cut. The bath and the iodine stung her owl scratch really badly, but Annie didn't cry. She was glad Daddy was getting all the owl claw germs out of it. It took five bandaids side by side to cover the long scratch. Daddy put iodine and a bandaid on the cut on her hand, too. And white lotion on her mosquito bites.

They got clean clothes out of Annie's drawer and Daddy helped her dress. He was very careful of the owl scratch.

"Why don't you rest a little while with your kittens," Daddy said. "You didn't get much sleep last night. You must be tired."

He led her to her bed. She lay down. She *was* tired. She curled around Misty and the kittens. Her bed and her pillow were so soft and comfy.

Daddy kissed her. "I'll be right downstairs," he said. "You're safe now."

✥

Meg stood in the kitchen a moment listening to Jesse's footsteps on the stairs as he carried Annie away from her. His words echoed in her mind, "I think it's best that I take care of her now." Her hand still felt Annie shrinking away from her touch. She turned into the dining room, dropped into a chair and buried her face in her arms on the table. Her head spun and ached.

She was aware of Donny standing near her, unusually quiet. He'd returned half an hour earlier and told her that Jesse had found Annie. He'd said she came crawling out from under a tree, had stood up to go to Jesse and fallen, but Jesse had caught her. Meg realized she hadn't seen Annie stand or walk. Had she been terribly injured some way Meg still didn't know about?

"Mama." She felt Donny's small hand on her shoulder. "It's okay now. Annie's home. Are we gonna go to the store? Daddy said we could take the car."

Meg struggled to get control of herself. He was calling her mama as he used to. Slowly she lifted her head. "Yes, we should go. Give me a minute. I need to get ready."

She pushed back her chair and stood. She was so stiff. Everything ached. She pulled on the railing to climb the stairs. At the top she paused. The door to the children's room was open. Misty and two kittens lay on the pink towel on Annie's bed. The bathroom door was shut. She could hear water running in the tub and Jesse talking softly to Annie.

Meg still didn't know which kittens she had drowned. She tiptoed into the children's room and peeked at the kittens. A gray one and a yellow one. The tiger, the dark gray one and Dapple were gone. Dapple. Meg felt a burning pang in her heart. She'd drowned Dapple, Annie's favorite. She hadn't even looked at which kittens she was grabbing.

She turned away and crossed the hall to her room, changed her dress and combed her hair. She badly wanted to wash her face, but didn't dare go into the bathroom.

Downstairs she found the car key and the wallet. There were fifty dollars in the wallet. She caught her breath at such abundance. She took twenty. That with the twenty-seven dollars in her purse would be plenty to buy everything she wanted.

Donny was waiting for her on the front steps. He jumped up and ran ahead of her to the car. "Can I ride on the running board? Daddy lets me sometimes."

"No," Meg answered. "Daddy shouldn't. It's too dangerous."

"Just down the driveway."

"Okay, just down the driveway, then you need to get inside."

The morning was already hot. It was such luxury to drive, not to have to walk the mile to the village in the heat. Donny had rolled down his window and the moving air felt good on her face. She rolled her window down, too. The car hummed along carrying her effortlessly to the store. Something softened within her. Maybe things really were going to be better.

In the store, Donny was excited. When she put some eggs in the basket, he said, "Can we get some bacon, too? At Grandma's we had bacon *and* eggs for breakfast. And jelly on our toast. Can we get some jelly? I like strawberry best."

So she got strawberry jam and bacon. She was excited, too, to be able to get things she had considered impossible luxuries for months, but her old habits of frugality warred with her desire to fill the basket with goodies. She bought only two cans of tuna fish, one bag of cat food, one loaf of bread, a half gallon of milk, some crackers and peanut butter and cheese, fruit and salad makings. The little grocery in Woodsborough didn't have much selection, but the produce was local and fresh. She didn't buy the chicken after all, because Jesse had said something about going to Boston right away.

When they checked out, Donny picked up one of the bags. "Daddy told me to help you."

Meg was so touched she felt weepy. Donny was a good boy, but had never been much into helping, and Meg had been too impatient to teach him.

When she got home, she found Jesse asleep on the couch, sprawled on his back, one arm across his eyes. Seeing him asleep like that made her realize how weary she was, but she was also excited to prepare a good breakfast for the family.

When all was ready—fresh blueberries, bacon and eggs, and toast with jam, she woke Jesse and sent Donny to get Annie. She followed him up the stairs to use the toilet and finally wash her face.

As she neared the top of the stairs, she heard Donny exclaim, "Hey, there's only two kittens. Where're the other three?"

Meg froze. Her hand gripped the railing. Her breath stopped. Would Annie tell him? Donny had just been so sweet and helpful. If he knew what she had done, he would hate her.

Annie didn't answer.

Donny insisted. "There were five. What happened to the other ones?"

In the silence that followed his question, Meg felt a wave of dizziness and feared she might faint. She gripped the railing tighter.

Finally Annie answered, her voice low. "They died."

"Died! How come they died? What happened to them?"

"They just died."

"But where are they? Where're their bodies?"

"I buried them. Up in the woods."

"Oh. Are the other two okay?"

"I think so."

Meg trembled with relief. Annie hadn't told on her. She could have taken terrible revenge. But she hadn't. Meg stepped quickly up the last few stairs and across the landing into the bathroom.

Before she shut the door, she heard Donny say, "Don't cry. Come on downstairs now. We have eggs and bacon for breakfast and jam for our toast. And Daddy's here."

Annie sat quietly at breakfast. She kept her eyes down except for peeking at Mama from time to time. Mama had combed her hair, but she still looked kind of bad. Even though she was acting gentle, Annie felt wary. There was a jagged feeling around Mama. Anyway Annie didn't want to talk to her. So she just ate. She was still hungry, even after the stew in the woods, and everything tasted really good. She loved strawberry jam.

Misty was eating, too. Annie had looked into the kitchen before she sat down and saw Misty crunching over her bowl of cat food. Annie peeked at Daddy. It made her feel good inside just to see him. He offered her a second piece of toast. She nodded. He was watching the toaster and turning it in time, so the toast wasn't even burned. The second piece—Daddy put lots of jam on it—filled her tummy right up.

Mama was being quiet. Daddy was taking charge.

"I've been making a plan," he said. "After breakfast we're all going to rest a while, because we've had a hard night. While you were at the store, I called Aunt Nellie, and this afternoon I'm going to take you children over to Grandma's to stay a few days while Mama and I go to Boston to find us a house. Then when we come back, we'll get a moving truck and move all our things up to our new home."

"We're going to move again?" Donny asked. "Aw, I don't wanna move. I'll have to leave all my friends and go to a new school again. I hate going to a new school."

"I'm sorry, son," Daddy said. "I know it's hard to leave your friends. But I have a job up in Boston and we can all be together again. You'll make new friends."

Annie didn't mind that they were going to move. She didn't have any friends. As long as Daddy was with them, it would be okay. And Misty and the kittens. But she felt sorry for Donny. She knew he really liked Jack.

Donny pushed back his chair. "I don't want to go to Grandma's. Mr. Martin has tomorrow off and him and me and Jack are going to work on the tree house all day."

"He and I," Mama said automatically.

"He and I," Donny repeated. "Can I go over to Jack's now? I don't wanna rest. I'm not tired. I need to tell Mrs. Martin we found Annie. And I wanna see Jack. He'll be mad I'm moving. Can I, Ma?"

Mama looked over at Daddy. "He did sleep last night. Let's let him go."

"All right," Daddy said to Donny. "But listen for the noon whistle and come home for lunch when you hear it."

"Okay." Donny's voice sounded funny like he was trying not to cry. He went straight out through the kitchen. The screen door banged behind him, and a moment later Annie heard his bike tires crunching on the driveway.

"It's too bad taking him away from working on the treehouse," Mama said. "He's been excited about it."

"It *is* too bad," Daddy replied. "But we need to go right away so we can find a house and get settled before school starts. How about you, Annie? Are you okay to go to Grandma's for a few days while Mama and I look for a house?"

Annie looked only at Daddy. Not Mama. "I'm okay. But I need to take Misty and the kittens."

"Of course," Daddy said. "I told Aunt Nellie about Misty and her babies and she said it was fine for them to come."

When Daddy said that, Mama twisted her head around real fast and looked at him with that fear look in her eyes.

She doesn't want Aunt Nellie to know she killed the kittens, Annie realized. She's scared Daddy told Aunt Nellie.

Daddy shook his head just a little and Mama made a little sigh. Annie knew then Daddy hadn't told on Mama. An odd feeling came over her. She could tell Aunt Nellie. That would hurt Mama. She had a secret that could hurt Mama. She could make her sorry for killing the kittens. It was a hot feeling spreading inside her.

The phone rang. Daddy went to answer it. Annie didn't like being alone with Mama. She started to slide out of her chair, then stopped to listen.

She heard Daddy saying, "That's very kind of you. I'm sure he would like that … Yes, she's okay. We're happy to have her home again. Please thank your husband for coming to look for her. And thank you for the stew. It's delicious … Yes, send him on home for lunch and we'll pack a bag for him and bring him back this afternoon."

Daddy talked a few more minutes, then came back into the dining room. Annie stood beside her chair where she had been poised to run if Mama got jagged. She was scared Mama somehow knew her thoughts and would hit her if she guessed Annie might tell on her to Aunt Nellie.

Daddy came and stood beside Mama. "Mrs. Martin invited Donny to stay with them while we go to Boston. That's good. They'll have time together before we leave."

Mama was still sitting in her chair leaning her elbows on the table like she always told Annie and Donny not to do. Daddy put his arm around her shoulders. "Go rest now," he said. "I'll clean up." He bent and kissed her cheek.

Mama got up. As she passed Annie, she touched Annie's hair. It was her gentle touch, but Annie pulled away and didn't look at her. She glanced up at Daddy. He was watching her with a frown on his forehead. Mama went out of the room and Annie heard her climbing slowly up the stairs.

Daddy sat down and drew Annie into his lap. "Are you okay to go to Grandma's all by yourself without Donny?"

"I'm okay."

Daddy held her close. "Of course you are. I forget how big and brave you've become, fending off owls and whacking raccoons with your big stick. Grandma and Aunt Nellie had better watch out."

Annie giggled.

Daddy set her out of his lap and took her hand. "Come now. Let's go upstairs. I want you to rest some more. You had a pretty wild night."

"Will you lie down with me?"

"Just for a little while. Then I need to clean up the kitchen and talk with Mama. Let's go see how Misty and the kittens are doing."

They went upstairs together. The door to Mama's room was closed. Misty had finished eating and was curled up with Dusty and Buttercup, nursing them. Daddy led Annie to the bed. She lay down beside her kitties. Daddy lay down on her other side and gathered her close in the curve of his arm.

Daddy was so big and warm. It felt so good to have him hold her. She sighed and began to feel sleepy. Then pictures of being on the ledge in the night started moving behind her eyes.

"Daddy."

"Yes."

"I didn't know stars gave enough light for you to see."

"They do. It's a dim light, but it does let you see some."

"And I didn't know the moon made shadows."

"Yes. Moon shadows have a different feel from sun shadows, don't they? I've always thought starlight and moonlight were kind of magical."

Annie liked that word. "I think they're magical, too." Then a shiver ran through her. "I'm really glad the moon does make shadows, or I wouldn't have seen the owl diving after Misty."

At the memory of that moment, panic pulsed through Annie's body and she tensed all over. She turned her head to look at Daddy. "That was scary."

Daddy held her closer. "I'm sure it was. But you saved Misty. See, she's right here beside you."

Annie's body softened again. Misty *was* right there. Annie could hear her purring while she nursed her kittens. Suddenly Annie was so tired. She barely felt it when Daddy kissed her and went away.

※

Meg dropped down on her bed and curled on her side. She knew she should rest, but her whole body hummed with tension. Jesse had pulled himself together, found Annie, and been kind and gentle with Meg, but she knew there was a reckoning coming.

And Annie. Meg had been so relieved to see her walking into the dining room for breakfast. Her legs hadn't been damaged after all. She was wearing a clean sunsuit, her hair had been washed and was still damp, and the scratch on her shoulder was carefully bandaged. There were white dots of calamine lotion on her face and arms. Jesse had taken good care of her.

Except for the scratch, she looked whole. But very tired. Thin. She had always been too thin for a little girl, especially during the last months of meager food. Now the twenty-four hours of fasting in the woods had pared her down even more, sharpening the angles in her little face. What had happened to her up there in the woods? She'd been scratched by an owl? How on earth …?

Meg rolled onto her back and flung her arm across her eyes.

There was a hardness in Annie she'd never felt before. Annie had always been so sweet, so docile, so eager to please, so quick to forgive Meg's storms and come back to Meg's embrace. But now she would not even let Meg touch her. The pain of that felt more than Meg could bear. Annie had not spoken a word to Meg or looked at her since Jesse brought her home. Except for that one glance when Jesse spoke of telling Nellie about Misty and the kittens. Jesse's little shake of the head had reassured Meg he had not told Nellie about her murderous act, but Annie's look in that moment had been one of pure hatred.

She had not told Donny. Would she tell Nellie? That would be disastrous.

Meg flipped to her side, and her dress wound around her. The one she'd put on clean and fresh to go to the store. She'd better take it off or she'd get it all wrinkled. She got up, took off her dress, hung it on the chair beside the bed, and lay down again in her bra and panties. A light breeze came through the open window, cooling her.

I should try to sleep, she told herself.

But she couldn't sleep.

A memory arose of a scene that had taken place in Mama and Nellie's big house before the move to Woodsborough. It had been a difficult time for Meg. Jesse's family was always interfering with how Meg was managing the children, giving abundant, unwanted advice. Jesse's mother had just been telling her how important it was to keep the children on a regular schedule. Overwhelmed with rage and frustration, Meg had fled to the library, a room in the house that was rarely used. She'd thought she was alone, but soon realized Annie was there. She was walking beside the bookcase, playing some imaginary game, chanting a little song under her breath as she touched the spines of the books one by one.

She looked up and saw Meg. In a flash, Meg saw her assess her mother's mood and sidle toward the door. Shame piled on top of Meg's frustration and she completely lost control of herself.

She had grabbed Annie by the arm and began striking her—across her face, her legs, her tiny bottom, her chest, whatever part of her came to hand as she struggled in Meg's grip. With each blow Meg had belted out her rage. "This is for your grandma, this is for your aunt Nellie, this is for your uncle Walter, and your aunt Sadie, and your uncle Don …" Usually Annie just sobbed when Meg struck her, but this was too much for her. She began screaming.

Chapter Eight — 123

The door of the library burst open and Nellie strode in. She was a small woman but had a big presence. "Stop that!" she shouted. She snatched Annie away from Meg and picked her up. Annie sobbed into her shoulder.

"You must learn to control yourself, Margaret," Nellie said in a voice of steel. "You will harm the child. I'll take her until you can pull yourself together."

After that Nellie had been civil but cold to Meg and began keeping Annie with her as she went about her household chores. Meg writhed on the bed as she remembered. Of course Nellie had been right to intervene. Annie had done nothing wrong; she had just been there, the handy object for Meg's rage. Meg still burned with shame and grief over what she had done that day.

As far as Meg knew, Nellie hadn't told Jesse what she'd witnessed, but after that Meg couldn't bear to stay any longer in the big house under the shadow of Mama and Nellie's judgment. So Jesse had found the Woodsborough house and the job on the road crew. Over the last year, helped by distance, relations between Meg and Nellie and Jesse's mother had eased. Meg was grateful that Nellie had sent the doll for Annie's birthday.

But now, if Annie told Nellie that Meg had drowned her kittens that tenuous relationship would be lost, probably for good.

The door opened and Jesse came in. He moved quietly to the bed and lay down beside her. Meg reached out a hand to him. He turned and took her in his arms.

"Are you still angry at me?" she asked.

He sighed. "Not so much angry now, but deeply concerned, not only about the kittens but also about the bruise on Annie's cheek. You must have slapped her hard to leave such a mark." He set her back from him a little and looked into her face. His voice was stern. "Your violence toward her has got to stop. She is a gentle, sensitive child, and from all I've seen only wants to be good and do what is asked of her. She does *not* need corporal punishment, especially when you lose control of yourself. If she needs correction, words are enough, and words spoken calmly."

"I know. You're right." Guilt and despair twisted inside her, twisted her body away from him. Overcome by his use of the word "violence," coupled with the recent memory of the scene in the library, she hid her face in her pillow.

"I'm glad you agree with me," Jesse said. "This has to end. I don't want to be afraid to leave the children with you, to come home and find them bruised in body and spirit. Because you know, I'm sure, that your blows have more than a physical effect. Can you promise you won't strike the children anymore?"

Could she promise? She didn't know. If she couldn't control herself, would he take the children away from her? She was silent, still turned away from Jesse. Finally she spoke, her voice muffled in the pillow. "I'll try. I don't know what's wrong with me. I didn't used to be so bad. But this last year has been so hard. Staying with Mama and Nellie, then here with you gone. With no money for food or anything. The children are outgrowing their clothes. And school starts in September."

"I'm sorry it's been so hard for you. You should have told me you and the children needed food and clothes."

Anger flared. He was right. She should have told him. He was always right, damn him.

"Why didn't you tell me?" he asked.

Why hadn't she? She swung around to face him. "Because I'd given up, that's why. Because you kept promising to send money, and never did. What could you do?"

"If I'd known you and the children were hungry, I'd have borrowed some money. Probably from Walter."

"Wish I'd known that." With a swift twist, she turned away from him again, and curled into a fetal position.

For what seemed like a long time, they lay there silent. She could hear his breath, feel the warmth of him close beside her and at the same time felt irrevocably separated from him, wrapped in the icy cocoon of her despair.

Then she felt him shift on the bed, felt the touch of his hand on her bare back.

"Don't go away Meg. We'll handle this together. I'll help you. I know much of this situation is my fault for not being with you when you needed me, for not providing well. But I'm here with you now, and I'm not leaving you again. I've got a good job, and I intend to keep it. Things are going to be better now."

He turned her over gently and held her again. "Let's rest while we can. We'll have time to talk more in the next few days."

She lay stiff in his arms.

"Do you realize," he went on "we're going to have a vacation together, just us, for the first time since Donny was born? And we'll find a house that you love." Gradually her body softened. In spite of everything, it felt so comforting to have him hold her.

He stroked her hair. "Let's sleep now for a little while. I'm exhausted and you are, too. And we have a big day ahead."

Rivulets of relief trickled through Meg. Maybe it was really going to be better. Maybe he loved her and would be patient and faithful to her as he had always been. And she would get control of herself. Somehow. She must. She laid her head on his shoulder and slept.

Chapter 9

Annie woke to the sound of footsteps coming into the bedroom. She opened her eyes and saw Mama standing at the end of her bed. In one swift move she rolled to sitting and pressed herself up against the wall at the head of her bed. Her heart pounded. Every fiber of her body tensed.

Dusty and Buttercup lay sleeping on the pink towel close to where she had been lying. Annie snatched up towel and kittens and held the precious bundle close against her chest, so tightly that one of the kittens squealed. Mama was only the length of the bed away. She had a basket in her hand, the same basket she had wanted to give Annie for the kittens before.

"It's okay, Annie," Mama said. "I didn't mean to startle you." It was her gentle voice, but she didn't feel gentle to Annie. Her eyes were pushing forward and her face was all pale. "I brought you a basket for your kittens," she said.

She came closer and set the basket on the bed. "I put a clean towel in. See? A green one to match Misty's green eyes."

Annie cast a quick glance around. Misty wasn't there. Mama was still talking. She took a step closer to Annie. "Would you like me to help you settle them?"

Annie scrunched harder against the wall and pulled the towel up under her chin. She could feel a tiny, soft head against her jaw. She was shaking inside, scared, really scared. And also mad, madder than she'd ever felt in her whole life. She sucked in her breath and spat out, "Don't. touch. my. kittens."

Mama stepped back. She was getting jagged, but Annie was too mad to care. "Go away," she said.

Mama's eyes flashed. "Don't talk to your mama that way."

Something swelled inside Annie. She was beyond caution. Words burst out of her. "You're not my mama. You're a wicked witch, just pretending to be my mama. You call me wicked, but *you* are wicked. I don't scream at people and hit them and *I don't kill babies*. I hate you. You killed my kittens and they'll never ever be alive again."

Mama took another step back. Annie saw her swell up the way she did before she hit. It looked just like the swelling Annie felt inside herself. Mama was taking little short breaths, just like Annie's. They stared at each other. Annie felt her eyes pushing forward just like Mama's.

Mama let out a long breath. "All right. I'll go now. Get your kittens settled and then come down to lunch." She turned and left the room.

Annie drew in a ragged breath. She wanted to cry, but she didn't. She needed to take care of her kittens. She laid the pink towel down on the bed and unwrapped it. With the tip of her finger she stroked each kitten. "I'm sorry I squeezed you," she said softly. "Are you okay?"

The kittens looked okay. Annie's heart swelled with love and tears came to her eyes. "I'm going to take good care of you," she told them. "Let's get you settled in your new basket. See, Mama put a clean towel in it for you." Gently she picked up Buttercup, kissed her and laid her in the basket. "You are so pretty and golden," she whispered, giving Buttercup another fingertip caress. "And you are pretty, too, Dusty." She gathered Dusty up, brushed her lips against Dusty's soft, gray fur and laid him down next to Buttercup.

Annie could smell stew smell coming up the stairs. She wondered what else Mama had fixed for lunch. She was hungry, but now her mad was gone and she was scared of what she had said to Mama. She was trembling all over and her tummy was flipping around. She didn't dare go downstairs. Instead she curled up on the bed, wrapping her body around the basket.

Meg stacked the last pan in the drainer and wiped down the counter. She was alone in the kitchen. Jesse had gone to visit their landlord and tell him they wouldn't be renewing their monthly lease in September. She'd sent Annie and Donny upstairs to pack for their visits, after giving Donny instructions and asking him to help Annie. She stood a moment, leaning against the refrigerator. Even though she'd slept a little that morning, she was still achingly weary, and still reverberating from Annie's harsh words.

She'd put them out of her mind while fixing lunch for the family. It had felt so good to have enough to prepare them a healthy, nourishing meal. She'd warmed up the rest of Ada's stew, made cheese sandwiches and a big salad, and served Annie's birthday cake for desert. She'd had to send Jesse up to bring Annie down. During the meal, Annie had been silent, eyes lowered, as she had been at breakfast, but she had eaten well.

Meg sighed and straightened. She'd better go up and see how the children were doing with their packing.

As she neared the top of the stairs she heard the children talking, and paused.

Danny said, "Your cheek's turning all purple. Did Mama hit you there?"

Annie's voice, low. "Yeah."

"Is that why you stayed up in the woods all night?"

"No. She hit me long ago. Before my birthday."

"Does it still hurt?"

"A little."

"Annie, you gotta learn to duck. I'll teach you. Let's practice. I'll pretend to hit you—I won't really. You duck."

"If she hits me again ..." Annie's voice had that new, fierce tone. "I'll hit her back."

"No! Don't do that. She's bigger'n you. That would make her really mad. You gotta learn to duck. Like this." Meg heard a thump and imagined Donny jumping.

She tiptoed up the last steps and looked in through the open door.

The two were standing at the foot of their beds, the only clear space in their small room. Donny moved. "Okay, I'm coming at you." He swung his arm. Annie ducked.

"No. Not quick enough. I coulda got you. Try again. Duck and then jump sideways. Like this."

Meg caught her breath as she saw him execute a move she recognized. No wonder she never connected. He was quick.

Donny swung his arm again. Annie moved more quickly this time, ducked, jumped sideways, and dived under Donny's bed. Donny squatted down and looked underneath. "That was better. Going under things is good, but then you're kind of stuck there. Let's try the sideways jump again. She always misses when I do that. But then you gotta run—fast—cause she gets madder when she doesn't get you. Of course, the best thing is to get far away when you see her getting mad. Just disappear."

Meg turned away, retreated down a few stairs and dropped to sitting, hunched over her knees, her face in her hands. It had come to this. One of her children teaching the other how to avoid her blows. As if they were to be expected. Hot shame poured through her. She rocked back and forth. How had she gotten so out of control? Annie had called her a witch. She'd planned to be a better mother than her own mother, but she was worse. What would her children say about her when they were grown? Her shame felt unbearable.

She heard more jumping sounds from upstairs. She took a deep breath, stood and gripped the handrail to steady herself, then started up the stairs again, calling ahead, "Donny, Annie, how's the packing coming?"

She came to their room. Suitcases were open on their beds. On Annie's bed, the pink towel lay rumpled beside the kittens' basket. Dirty, but not torn, she noted with relief. As soon as she entered, Annie scrambled onto her bed, pressed up against the wall, and pulled the basket into her lap.

"We're all done," Donny said. "We got in everything you told us—toothbrush and hair brush and comb, underwear and socks for four days, a sweater, pajamas and clothes."

"Good for you." Meg went and looked into the suitcases. Donny's looked fine. He hadn't packed his teddy bear, she noticed. Annie's had the required toilet articles and underwear, her nightgown, three dresses and no long pants. Her two reading books were also there, and Misty's ball.

"You don't need three dresses," Meg said to her. She felt sick, seeing Annie's fear, the way she pressed up against the wall and clutched the basket.

"Grandma wants me to wear dresses," Annie said. Her voice was low. She didn't look at Meg.

"Yes. That's right. I forgot." Meg remembered that Jesse's mother thought little girls shouldn't wear pants. "It's okay to take them. But let's put in your overalls, too, in case Uncle Don wants to take you down to the farm."

"My overalls are dirty. Daddy put them in the laundry bag."

"Oh." Meg sighed. She went to Annie's dresser. "Then let's pack your slacks, even though they're a little short for you now." She took out the slacks and laid them in Annie's suitcase.

Donny was still in the room, shifting from one foot to the other. Meg turned to him. "Go on downstairs now. I want to talk to Annie alone for a few minutes."

Donny gave Annie a warning glance and left, thumping down the stairs, a jump at the bottom.

Chapter Nine • 131

Annie had shrunk farther against the wall at the head of her bed, clutching the basket against her chest. Her eyes were wide and wary, gauging Meg's every move.

Meg sat down on the end of the bed. She was shaking inside with grief, and, yes, she was scared, too. She longed to gather her frightened child into her arms and comfort her.

Her voice trembled in spite of herself. "Annie, please don't be so afraid of me. I won't hurt you, or Buttercup or Dusty. I'm very very sorry …" She couldn't bear to say "I killed." She hesitated. "About the other three. It was a terrible mistake. I was afraid we didn't have enough food for so many kittens. I wanted to have food for you and Donny. But what I did was wrong. I wish I hadn't."

Annie stared at her, her eyes filled with fear, anger, grief. Meg's stomach roiled and contracted. What a terrible cocktail of emotions she had evoked in her precious little girl.

"They weren't just 'so many kittens,'" Annie said, her voice low but fierce. "They were Tiger, Smokey, and Dapple. They were *my* kittens and I loved them."

"I know. I'm very sorry. I wish I hadn't done it. I want you to know I'm not going to hurt Dusty and Buttercup."

"Promise?"

"I promise." Meg took a deep breath and made another promise. "And I'm not going to hit you anymore. You're right. That's wicked. Can we be friends again? Will you talk to me? I want to know about the owl and what happened to you up in the woods all night."

"I'm sorry I tore your basket. I didn't mean to." Annie had lowered her eyes and wasn't looking at Meg anymore.

"I know you didn't." Meg held out her arms. "May I hold you?"

Annie's eyes lifted to flash Meg one quick look of fear. She contracted farther into herself and shook her head.

Her rejection smacked Meg like a blow across the face. Fearing she might cry, she stood up hastily and left the room.

Annie sat in the front seat of the car next to Daddy. Usually Mama sat there and Annie and Donny sat in the back seat. But Mama was still at home and Donny had ridden his bike to Jack's house.

She and Daddy were driving to Jack's house to take Donny's suitcase and return the stew pot. Annie's suitcase and Misty and the kittens in their basket were in the back seat, because right after they took the things to Jack's house they were going to Grandma's. Misty had cried when the car started, but Annie had held her close and told her it was okay, then put her back with her babies. She was sitting up in the basket, looking anxious but not crying anymore. Annie turned around to tell her again that it was okay.

It didn't take long to get to Jack's house. His house was even littler than Annie and Donny's house, but it had pretty red and yellow flowers growing by the front door. Daddy got out with the suitcase and the pot, and Jack's mama came to the door. They talked for a while. Annie stayed in the car.

She could see into the back yard and could see the big tree with the tree house that Donny had told her about. Jack and Donny were up in the tree. Donny had already said good-bye to her, but she wished he would come out of the tree and say good-bye again. She was feeling kind of funny going to Grandma's all by herself, even though she'd told Daddy it was okay.

Daddy was quiet as they turned out of the side street where Jack lived and drove through the village. They passed the school, one of the churches, some houses and the factory. There was lots of dark gray smoke coming out of the chimneys. Annie felt sad thinking about Smokey. And Dapple and Tiger.

She got up on her knees and looked over into the back seat. Misty had lain down with Dusty and Buttercup, but still held her head up and looked uneasy.

"Misty doesn't like riding in the car," Annie said.

Daddy nodded. "Most cats don't, but she's not crying anymore. That's good." Annie reached across the back of the front seat, stretched as far as she could, and was just able to touch Misty's head. "It's okay, Misty," she said. "We're going to a new place, but we'll be safe there. There'll be no wild animals. And I'll be with you and help you take care of your babies."

Misty looked up at Annie, purred briefly, then laid her head down.

Annie sat down again next to Daddy. "She's okay. I'll put her basket right by my bed at Grandma's house."

"That's a good idea," Daddy said. "I think we should put her litter box and her food and water dishes in the room with you, too. That will help her to be comfortable, give her a sense of her territory. Cat's like to have their territory. I'll arrange that with Aunt Nellie."

Annie gave a little sigh and sat closer to Daddy. She loved him so much. He always understood.

They rode in silence for a while. Then Daddy said, "You didn't say good-bye to Mama."

Annie didn't say anything. When she thought of Mama, she could still feel the hot mad inside.

"Are you still scared of her?" Daddy asked.

Annie thought about it. "Not so much."

"What changed?"

"She promised she wouldn't hurt Dusty and Buttercup." Annie realized that was what she'd been most scared of. Last night, with the bad dream, she'd been scared Mama might drown her, but now she knew Mama wouldn't do that.

"How about you. Are you afraid she might hurt you?"

"She said she wouldn't hit me anymore. She didn't promise. But Donny taught me how to dodge."

"He did, did he?" Daddy's voice sounded funny, like he might be trying not to laugh. "Well, I'm glad you're not so scared. But I think you're still angry. Is that why you wouldn't let Mama hug you goodbye?"

"Uh huh."

"That made Mama sad."

"I don't care."

Daddy didn't say anything for a while. Annie felt kind of sick in her tummy. She knew Daddy didn't like what she'd said.

Then Daddy said, "Mama loves you lots. Do you know that?"

Annie wanted to tell Daddy about gentle Mama and the wicked witch but was afraid to. Her tummy felt all wiggly inside and she couldn't say anything. Daddy didn't say anything either. They were on the big road now, and there weren't any houses. Annie looked out the window at the fields and trees passing by.

After a long time, Daddy asked, "*Do* you know your mama loves you?"

"Sometimes." Annie's wanting to tell him about the gentle mama and the wicked witch became stronger than the wiggles in her tummy. Her words suddenly tumbled out. "Sometimes Mama is gentle and then I think she loves me. But sometimes she turns into a wicked witch and hits me and screams at me and scares me. Then she hates me. I know she does."

"Ah, Annie." Daddy sounded sad. "Your mama's not a witch. She doesn't ever hate you. She gets scared sometimes when things get out of control."

Annie thought about that. What was out of control? Annie staying too long in the woods? Misty having five kittens? Not enough money for food? She didn't want to ask Daddy. She just said, "When I get scared I want to run away and hide. I don't hit."

"People do all sorts of things when they're scared. Hitting is one of them, but not a good choice. This war that's going on—it's lots of scared people hitting each other, but because they have bombs and guns they are killing each other. It's a terrible thing."

Daddy sounded even sadder. Annie knew the war was bad, but she didn't like to think about it. She didn't want to think about her mama being scared, either. If grown-ups could be scared, then nothing was safe. She looked out the window again. They were getting near a town; there were more houses.

"Tell me what your mama is like when she is gentle," Daddy said.

Annie didn't want to talk about gentle Mama. She wanted to stay mad. So she didn't say anything.

Daddy looked over at her. "Later maybe. We're almost to Grandma's house."

Annie recognized the road that turned off the big road. It wound between fields that had cows in them, then past the farm with the farmhouse, the big barn, and all the pens with chickens and goats and pigs. There was a yellow cat sitting in front of the farm house. Like the cat that was the daddy of Misty's kittens. The road went on by the farm and up the big hill to Grandma's house at the top.

Chapter 10

Annie sat up straight and gripped the door handle when Daddy pulled the car up in front of Grandma's big house. Her heart started beating faster. Aunt Nellie was sitting in a rocking chair on the porch, reading. As soon as she saw them, she dropped her book and came running down the steps to meet them.

Daddy got out of the car and Aunt Nellie hugged him. "Jesse, it's good to see you. It's been so long." She stepped back a little to look into his face and put her hand up to touch his cheek.

Aunt Nellie was much older than Daddy. Daddy had a little white hair mixed in with his dark hair at the sides of his forehead, but Aunt Nellie's hair was white almost all over. It was in braids wrapped around her head. Annie liked that. Sometimes she wished she had hair long enough to make braids, but Mama always cut it short so it would curl more.

Aunt Nellie came around to the other side of the car and opened the door. "There you are, Annie. Grandma and I are so glad you came to visit." She reached into the car, picked Annie up, and hugged her.

It felt nice to have Aunt Nellie hug her, but Annie was worried about Misty. She'd jumped up on the back of the front seat and looked as if she might run away. Annie wiggled free of Aunt Nellie's hug, climbed back in the car, caught Misty, and held her close against her chest.

"I need to take care of my kitties," she told Aunt Nellie. "Misty's worried."

"Of course," Aunt Nellie said. She looked into the back seat. "Two little babies. Aren't they sweet. Let's settle them in the back entry. There's a good corner for them there."

Misty was struggling in Annie's arms. The back entry. Annie got scared. "No …" she started to say. But Daddy spoke right up.

"Misty sleeps with Annie," he said. "It's important to her. I've promised her that Misty and the kittens will be in her room with her. We've brought Misty's food and dishes and litter tray and a tarp to go under them to protect the floor."

"But …" Aunt Nellie started to protest, but Daddy was firm.

"We'll get it all set up and Annie will take care of Misty. Let's take the kittens in right now before Misty gets more upset. I'll bring the basket." He had the basket in his hands and was starting up the porch steps. Annie held tight to Misty and followed him. Aunt Nellie trailed behind saying, "Well, maybe … I guess it will be all right. Mama won't like it."

"She doesn't need to know," Daddy said. "Which room will Annie be in?"

Aunt Nellie led them upstairs and down the hall. "Here we are. This is the same room you stayed in before when you and your mama and daddy and Donny lived with us. Do you remember?"

Annie nodded. She did remember. It was a long time ago. She had only been three then and didn't have Misty yet. She'd turned four and got Misty for her birthday just before they'd moved to Woodsborough.

Daddy put the basket on the bed. "Stay here with Misty," he said. "I'll bring up your suitcase and her things. Keep the door shut so she doesn't run away."

"I'll help you carry things," Aunt Nellie said. She and Daddy went out, closing the door behind them. Annie could hear their footsteps going away.

She took Misty over to the bed and put her in the basket with the kittens, then sat down beside her and looked around. It was a nice room, much bigger than the one she shared with Donny at home. It had two windows side by side with a big windowsill. Annie remembered that she used to sit there and look out at the sloping lawn and the trees behind the house. There was a low bureau with a mirror on top, a little desk the right size for Annie, and a chair. The bed had two pillows and a pretty blue and white bedspread.

Misty sniffed and licked her kittens. Then she looked up at Annie with a questioning meow. Annie stroked her head. "This is your new territory," she told Misty. "We'll be safe here. There's no owls or raccoons or foxes."

Annie knew they'd be safe, but the room felt too big and she really missed Donny.

Misty began exploring. Annie watched as she went all around the edges of the room, sniffing. She climbed on the windowsill and looked out for a while, went under the bed and came out again. Her ears were bent back a little, and Annie could tell she was still uneasy.

The door opened and Daddy and Aunt Nellie came in. Daddy had Annie's suitcase and the green tarp that he always took to cover the picnic table when they went camping. Aunt Nellie had the litter tray with Misty's dishes and food in it.

Daddy put Annie's suitcase by her bed and laid the tarp down in the corner by the window. "I need to get back to Meg," he said to Aunt Nellie. "Can you help Annie get unpacked and set things up for Misty?"

"Of course," Aunt Nellie said. "But can't you stop for a cup of tea before you go? Mama will want to see you."

"I'll say hello to Mama for sure, but no tea this time. It's a long drive to Boston and we need to get started if we're going to get there this evening. But I do want a word with you before I go."

Daddy and Aunt Nellie went out again, shutting the door behind them. Annie felt all alone. She decided to fix up Misty's corner. She didn't need Aunt Nellie to help her. She sat down on the tarp and took Misty's dishes and cat food out of the tray. She'd need to go down to the bathroom to get water for Misty's water dish, and put the bag of cat food away in a bureau drawer after she filled Misty's food dish, so Misty wouldn't tear the corner open like she'd done once.

Before she even started, a sudden chill went through her. Daddy hadn't said good-bye. He wouldn't leave without saying good-bye, would he? Had he already gone? She didn't want him to just go and leave her there. She jumped to her feet and ran out into the hall, leaving the food bag and dishes scattered across the tarp. Quickly, she turned back and shut the door so Misty would be safe.

Just down the hall was the spiral staircase with the smooth banister that she and Donny used to slide down. She ran to the top of the stairs. Daddy and Aunt Nellie were in the hall at the bottom, talking. Annie let out her breath. Daddy hadn't gone yet, but what was he saying?

"Please be very gentle with her," he said. "She's had a hard time."

"What happened?" Aunt Nellie asked.

"Misty had five kittens. Meg was worried about money. I didn't realize that she'd been scrimping to get together enough food for the children. The idea of six cats to feed overwhelmed her, so she drowned three of the kittens."

Annie crouched down behind the top railing of the staircase, shaking all over. *Daddy* was telling Aunt Nellie, even though Mama didn't want him to. Aunt Nellie would know, and Annie wouldn't be the one to tell her.

Daddy was still talking. "Unfortunately Annie had already become attached to all the kittens, had given them names. Even more unfortunately, unbeknownst to Meg, Annie witnessed the drowning. She became frightened, took Misty and the remaining two kittens, ran away into the woods behind our house, and stayed all night."

"Good Lord," Aunt Nellie exclaimed. "She was up in the woods all night? Alone?"

"Quite alone, and protecting Misty and the kittens from a fox, a raccoon, and an owl. The owl almost got Misty. Annie dived to protect her and the owl knocked her down and tore a deep scratch in her shoulder."

Aunt Nellie had her hand pressed against her chest. "Oh, my goodness. Poor child. She's so little."

"And very brave. Can you look after the wound, change the bandaids each day and be sure it doesn't get infected? It's quite painful for her."

"Of course I will."

"That's why it's so important that Misty and the kittens be with her. She was protecting them and very frightened. She needs the reassurance of having them close."

"I see. I understand. Of course we'll let the kittens stay with her. You're right. Mama doesn't need to know. We've made a room for her off the parlor now, since she has so much trouble with the stairs."

"That sounds like a good idea. I'm sorry. I haven't even asked about Mama. I've been so worried about Annie—and Meg. I'll go give Mama a kiss before I leave, and when we get back we'll stop for a longer visit. Where is she?'

"In her usual chair in the living room."

Daddy and Aunt Nellie left the hall. Annie stayed crouched at the top of the stairs. The floor was hard and cold, but she didn't move. Thoughts and feelings jumped around inside her so fast they bumped into each other. She could hardly breathe. Daddy told Aunt Nellie. Daddy was going to leave. She didn't want him to leave her alone at Grandma's. She didn't want Daddy to leave her ever again. She missed Donny. She missed Mama. No. She hated Mama. No. She wanted gentle Mama so bad it made her whole chest hurt.

She lay there a long time. Finally Daddy came back, running up the stairs two at a time. He stopped suddenly when he saw her and sat down beside her. She uncurled, climbed in his lap, and wrapped her arms tight around his neck.

She was crying. "Daddy, don't leave me. I don't want to stay here. Take me with you."

Daddy held her close. "I need to leave you for just a little while. Mama and I need to find a new house in Boston where we can all be together. We'll be back in just a few days, and then you'll go with us."

Annie was crying even harder. "Don't leave me." Huge sobs hurt her chest. Her nose was running and tears were getting her shirt all wet.

"Easy, sweetheart," Daddy said, smoothing her head. "We need to think about Misty and her babies. Misty doesn't like to travel. It's a long way to Boston and when we get there, we'll be riding all around looking for a house. It's best if you stay here with her. Aunt Nellie and Grandma will take good care of you. They're really glad you came to visit. And Misty and the kittens will be safe here."

Daddy's arms were warm around her. "I know it's been a lot of change for one day," he said. "But I need you to be brave again. Remember how strong you are. Raccoon's Bane."

Annie sucked up her sobs. "What's bane?"

"A terrible, dangerous thing. That's what you were to that raccoon. All he wanted was a nice kitty for dinner and what he got was a whack from mighty Annie."

Something about the way Daddy said that made a tiny giggle start in Annie's chest. She remembered whacking the raccoon with her stick. She *had* been strong. She had chased him away. She took a long trembling breath. Daddy wanted her to be brave. "Okay," she said. She looked up at him and put her hands on both sides of his face. "Promise you'll come back."

"I promise," he said, deep and serious.

Annie knew Daddy always kept his promises.

He stood up, still holding her in his arms. "Will you come out to the car with me and wave good-bye?"

Annie took another deep, raggedy breath. "Okay."

Daddy carried her down the stairs and set her on her feet. Aunt Nellie came and they went out to the car. Daddy hugged Aunt Nellie and picked Annie up again for one last hug and kiss. Then he got in the car. Annie waved. He waved back, threw her a kiss, and drove away.

Meg stood on the front steps watching Jesse and Annie drive away. Jesse had held her tight in his arms before they left. "I'll be back as soon as I get Annie settled. Get ready. I'm looking forward to our time together. I've missed you so much."

Annie had come downstairs with the kittens' basket and Misty following close behind her. She'd brushed by Meg without a glance or a word and run to the car. Pausing only to scoop up Misty, she'd climbed into the back seat and shut the car door. Meg had gone out to say goodbye, but Annie had turned away. As Jesse backed down the driveway, Meg saw her climb over the seat and settle in the front beside him.

Then they were gone.

Meg went back into the house. It felt empty and quiet in a way she hadn't experienced before. They were all gone, even the cat. She wouldn't see the children again for several days and nights—she didn't even know how long. She'd never been away from them for even one night since they were born, except for last night, the terrible night when Annie was up in the woods.

Meg walked into the dining room and sank down in a chair by the table. Donny had given her a quick hug before he rode away on his bicycle, but she could feel that he was already focused on his new adventure. And Annie …

No hug. Not even a word.

Meg felt a sob rising in her chest. She tried to reassure herself. Annie was barely five, still very young. She'd get over it. Would she? Meg wasn't sure. Even if she talked to Meg again, would she be irrevocably marked by Meg's blows, by seeing her drown the kittens?

Meg remembered her own mother's blows, the slaps across the face. The cold look in her mother's eyes. The little switch she'd used to strike the tender palm of Meg's hand. Meg still felt the grief, the injustice, the pain of that. And she was thirty-four.

She gave herself a shake. Jesse had said "Get ready." She must clean up, pack her suitcase, put the house in order. Damn! Annie's sheets were still in the washtubs behind the house. She couldn't leave them there.

Slowly she straightened and rubbed her brow. She pushed her chair back and strode through the kitchen and out the back door. The afternoon sun shone down hot on the washtubs. A kind of frenzy came over her. Just get it done. Fortunately most of the blood from Misty's birthing had soaked out, leaving the water a pale pink. Meg let the water out, ran fresh, put in soap, set up the washboard, and scrubbed. It didn't take long after all. Two rinses back and forth between the tubs. She wrung the sheets out and hung them on the line that was stretched from the shed to the nearest tree at the edge of the woods. She'd have to bring them in again before she left, but they could start drying there in the sun.

She stood a moment catching her breath. Now to pack. Upstairs in her bedroom she pulled her suitcase out from the back of the closet. Her good dress-up clothes hung there. She hadn't worn them since they moved to Woodsborough. Carefully she took down a yellow rayon dress with a flared skirt and puff sleeves, a light-weight tan suit, and a white blouse. She scooped up her heels from the back of the closet. From the top drawer of her dresser, she pulled out scarves, jewelry, underwear, silk stockings.

She caught a glimpse of herself in the mirror over the dresser. She was a mess. Her hair hung limply against her face. She hadn't had it cut for months, and the last job, by a local hairdresser, had left much to be desired. There were deep shadows under her eyes and streaks of sweat across her brow.

She'd be sure everything was in order, then have a shower and shampoo. Washing the sheets had taken the last of the hot water. She hurried downstairs to light the boiler, then went through the house room by room, closing the windows, tidying, putting away dishes in the drainer, wiping down the counters, making the beds. Maybe there was enough hot water now.

After a warm—not really hot—shower and shampoo, Meg felt better. She dressed carefully in a flowered skirt, a rose-colored blouse that she knew Jesse liked, and a rose quartz necklace. As she combed and coaxed her damp hair into waves, she felt a tingle of excitement. She was going on a trip with her dear husband, a date. She assessed herself in the mirror. Better, but she was still pale and the dark smudges under her eyes looked awful. Some powder to cover them and some lipstick. That helped a little.

When she was all dressed, she checked the contents of her suitcase, added her make-up, latched the suitcase and carried it downstairs. The sheets. She turned off the boiler, hurried out the back door, brought the sheets in, and took them upstairs to hang over the shower rail.

Ready at last, she collapsed into the big chair in the living room. She glanced at her watch. Ten after three. Jesse should be back soon. It was only a half hour drive to Mama's house. It would take some time to settle Annie and Misty and, of course, Mama would want a visit. Meg sighed, suddenly exhausted, and leaned her head against the back of the chair.

She couldn't stop thinking of Annie. She realized she was uncomfortable about Annie going to the farm. Would she bond to Nellie again and love her more than Meg?

Nellie was considered the saint of the family. She'd never married or had children of her own, but had helped bring up her five younger brothers—Jesse was the youngest of them—and then stayed on to care for her aging parents. Now it was just Nellie and Mama there in the big house on the hill, though the oldest brother, Don, lived close by and stopped by often to check on them and supervise the farm. Meg had to admit Nellie was a loving, generous person, but she didn't want to lose Annie to her in this precarious time.

How could Meg win Annie back? She had promised Annie she would never hit her again. Could she manage that? *Could* she control herself?

She remembered how she'd resolved when she became pregnant with Donny that she would be a better mother than her mother had been. Her own mother had mostly neglected her children. Except for rule making and discipline, she passed Meg and her brother off to one nursemaid after another. The nursemaids never lasted long, because Meg's mother was so difficult to work for. There was more attention for Meg's brother—the first born, the favored one—but even he was often physically punished and passed his anger on by hitting and tormenting Meg. Blows had been the language of relationship in her family. The habits and wounds were deep.

Meg *had* been a better mother than her mother. She had delighted in her babies, nursed them, played with them, sang to them, read to them, taught them. She'd studied books about childhood development and watched over all the children's stages. And she loved them. She'd done a lot of things right.

But the unremitting tasks of housework and childcare sometimes felt so draining, so confining. Nothing in her upbringing had prepared her for such a life. In spite of her mother's sternness, in spite of the restrictions of her strict Christian upbringing, Meg knew she'd been pampered. She'd never had to wash a dish or clean her room, even make her bed. Maids did all that. She'd known it would be a big change when she married Jesse and would have to do everything herself. Her love for Jesse made it all seem possible. So she'd learned and mostly done well.

But when she was weary and there seemed no end to the chores that lay before her, no break from the insistence of the children's needs, when she was frightened or stressed, then the old patterns of lashing out would reassert themselves.

Meg twisted in the chair. Shame swept over her again. She remembered Jesse's words, "bruised in body and spirit," and felt that her heart would break.

It was always easier when Jesse was with her. If only he could keep this new job, bring in enough money for them to be secure, and come home to her every night, maybe then she could overcome her impulsive violence.

No. She couldn't make it conditional on what Jesse did. It was *her* temper, her job to handle. A resolution that felt like steel formed within her. She *must* learn to control herself.

She had long ago turned away from her Christian upbringing, but now a prayer rose within her. "God help me," she whispered.

Aunt Nellie took Annie's hand. "Shall we go in now? Grandma would like to see you."

Annie still felt kind of raggedy from crying so hard, but she nodded and let Aunt Nellie lead her across the broad porch and into the house. Grandma was sitting in her chair in the living room. She was really old. Her white hair was thin and wispy and knotted up on the top of her head. Her whole body was thin and her blue eyes were faded. She held out her arms when Aunt Nellie and Annie came into the room.

"Annie, come here."

Annie remembered that when she was three she used to sit in Grandma's lap, but she couldn't do that now. Grandma's lap was too narrow, and Annie was afraid she would squish her. She went to Grandma's chair and Grandma reached out and put an arm around her. "How you've grown," Grandma said. "How are you?"

"Fine." But Annie didn't feel fine. Her chest still ached because Daddy was gone, and she was really, really tired. She wanted to sit down, but there was no place to sit down by Grandma's chair and Grandma still had her arm around Annie.

"Would you like to have a cup of tea and some cookies?" Aunt Nellie asked. "We could bring them in here and have a tea party with Grandma."

Annie felt weak in her tummy. The idea of a cookie made her feel sick. And she was worried about Misty because she remembered she hadn't filled Misty's dishes and there was no dirt in her litter box. "No, thank you," she said. "I want to go to my room and check on …" She stopped, remembering that Aunt Nellie had said Grandma wouldn't like her to have Misty and the kittens in her room. She looked up at Aunt Nellie. "I just want to go to my room."

Aunt Nellie seemed to know that she had almost given away the secret. "That's right. We haven't unpacked your suitcase yet. I'll come help you. Give Grandma a kiss. You'll see her again at dinner."

Annie kissed Grandma's cheek. It felt soft and wrinkly.

As Annie and Aunt Nellie climbed the stairs, Annie said, "I almost told, but then I remembered."

"I know. I'm glad you remembered."

Misty was on the bed with the kittens. She sat up, alert, when the door opened.

Annie went to her. "It's okay, Misty. It's just me and Aunt Nellie. There's no raccoons here."

Aunt Nellie laughed. "I should hope not."

"There was one. Last night in the woods."

"Your daddy told me. And he told me that you got scratched by an owl. You've had a big adventure. You'll be safe here, you and your kitties. Now let's get you unpacked and Misty's corner fixed up."

Aunt Nellie opened Annie's suitcase and hung her dresses in the closet. Annie put the rest of her clothes in the bureau except for her toothbrush, hairbrush, and comb, which she put on top. Together they filled Misty's water and food dishes, then went down the back stairs and out to the garden to fill the litter box. Aunt Nellie got a trowel from the shed to dig with.

When Annie saw the trowel, she thought of the one she'd used to dig up rocks for the fort, and then taken up to her cave to dig a grave for the dead kittens. And to break her stick off the tree. Then she got the feeling in her tummy that she got when she'd done something wrong. She'd left the trowel up by her cave. Mama would be mad. She always told Donny and Annie to put away their toys when they were done playing with them. As soon as she got home, she'd have to go and get it.

"I'd like you to dig up the dirt for the litter box," Aunt Nellie was saying. "It's hard for me to get down on my knees."

Annie felt confused for a moment. She had been back under the tree finding the trowel and now she was suddenly standing in Aunt Nellie's garden. The sun shone down hot on her head and she felt wobbly the way she'd felt that morning when she tried to stand up to go to Daddy. She sat down suddenly. Aunt Nellie handed her the trowel. Annie dug into the earth. It was much softer than the hard, rocky ground near Donny's fort and it smelled good. She felt better as she piled it into the litter box.

After they'd brought the litter box back in and put it on the tarp in the corner of Annie's room, Aunt Nellie said, "There now. You and Misty are all settled. Would you like to come down to the kitchen and help me make a pie for dinner?"

Annie's legs were all shaky and she felt like crying again. She sat down on the bed. "I want to stay here with Misty."

Aunt Nellie put her hand on Annie's forehead. "Are you feeling all right?"

"I'm just kind of tired."

Aunt Nellie sat down on the bed and gathered Annie into her lap. "Poor little one. You're all tuckered out. Being up in the woods alone all night must have been really scary. But you're safe now. Grandma and I are so glad you came to visit. We'll have a good time together." She rocked Annie back and forth and kissed her forehead.

Annie snuggled into Aunt Nellie's arms. She remembered that Aunt Nellie had always been kind to her. Aunt Nellie was safe. She never hit or yelled at Annie. Annie rested her head against Aunt Nellie's shoulder. She was so tired. Aunt Nellie was still rocking her. "Poor little one," she said again. "You need to rest now."

She moved and laid Annie down on the bed beside her kitties. Misty came and snuggled against her chest.

"Have a good rest," Aunt Nellie said. "I'll be in the kitchen if you need me. I'll come tell you when dinner is ready."

She stood looking at Annie for a moment, then bent and kissed her cheek.

☙ ❧

They were driving away from Woodsborough, leaving behind the little stone house and the difficult year Meg had endured there. The afternoon was hot, but the air blowing in through the open car windows was cooling and the sun was behind them as they traveled east.

Meg sat close to Jesse, drinking in his nearness. She rested her hand on his thigh. He laid a hand over hers and glanced over to smile at her.

"You look really nice," he said. "I like that color on you." He squeezed her hand. "I've missed you sorely."

A wave of emotion rose from Meg's chest and into her throat. Tears stung the back of her eyes. His dear voice. His dear hand touching hers. "I've missed you, too. So much." There were no words to say how much.

They rode a while in silence. Meg didn't want to break the sweetness of their intimacy, but she couldn't stop thinking of Annie.

"How did it go getting Annie settled?" she asked finally.

Jesse put his hand back on the wheel. "A bit rough. She cried and didn't want me to leave her, but then she found her inner resources and gave me a brave farewell. Nellie will take good care of her. I told her the whole story about Annie's night in the woods and the kittens."

"You didn't tell Nellie I drowned the kittens."

"I did. And that Annie had seen and was frightened."

"Oh, Jesse, no!" Meg pulled her hand away from his thigh and covered her face with both hands. "Why did you tell her that? She already judges me. Now I'll never be able to look her in the eye."

"I wanted her to understand how important it was for Misty and the kittens to be in Annie's room. Nellie was talking of putting them in the back hall. Meg, it's okay. Remember Nellie and I and our brothers grew up on a farm—pigs, goats, chickens, cattle. We know sometimes you need to cull a litter."

Meg shook her head in bewilderment. "Then why were you so angry with me?"

"Because you didn't attend to what culling the litter would do to Annie. She was attached to those kittens, so delighted with each one, thought it was magical that five kittens had been born on her fifth birthday. All that. If you'd found the kittens before she did and removed three, I'd have had no problem with that. I'm not so keen myself on having six cats underfoot. But to kill them after she'd fallen in love with each one, named them. And then that you didn't even look around to see that she was watching you."

"I never meant for her to see. Annie found the kittens first. They were born in the bottom of her bed."

"Which made it all the more special for her. There were other ways to handle it. We could have found homes for them. Let Annie enjoy them for a little while, explain to her, prepare her for letting them go. Tell her they would bring happiness to another child."

Nauseous with shame, Meg couldn't speak. She sat silent, her hands still covering her face. At last she spoke. "I know. I acted without thinking."

"Let it go now. Let's focus on helping Annie heal. And you, too. It's been hard for you as well."

"It has. I don't know if Annie will ever forgive me. She said terrible things to me, called me a wicked witch. And she will barely look at me, speak to me, much less let me touch her."

Meg began to cry. Jesse took one hand off the wheel and rested it on her thigh again.

"I love her so much," Meg sobbed. "I want her to love me."

"I know you love her. I told her that when we were on our way to Mama's. I asked her if she knew you loved her. She told me that sometimes you were a gentle mama and then she thought you loved her, but when you were a wicked witch she thought you hated her."

"Oh!" Meg's weeping intensified. "I never hated her. Only myself."

Jesse kept his hand on Meg's thigh. The road was straight with little traffic. The sun was low, the shadow of the car long in front of them.

Gradually Meg's sobs subsided. She searched in her purse for her handkerchief and blew her nose. "Annie is so changed," she said. "She never spoke to me like that before. She's always forgiven me, let me hold her and comfort her after …" She couldn't bear to say "after I hit her."

"Yes." Jesse nodded. "This whole event has changed her. She has found her voice, her outrage, her strength."

"I don't even know what happened to her up there all night. Did she tell you anything? How in the world did she tangle with an owl? I can't even imagine that."

"She told me the whole story as we sat by her cave while she ate her stew. The incident with the owl *was* extraordinary."

"Her cave? I don't know anything except how she looked when you brought her home all covered with blood and mosquito bites. Tell me."

Jesse shifted his leg to turn the headlights on. "She had many adventures up there in the woods. Many dangers and fears as well as wonders."

As they drove into the deepening dusk, he told her Annie's story. Meg listened with increasing amazement. "You said she was resourceful. She really was. Diving under the owl to protect Misty! That was dangerous."

"Yes. And brave. The owl marked her. It's been a huge initiation for her—like the ones certain primitive tribes put their young men through at puberty. But she is only five, and she not only had to take care of herself, but protect her kittens from wild animals. It's true. The little girl who ran away from you yesterday is not the same child who returned with me this morning."

Meg was suddenly exhausted thinking of Annie's night and her own night. Perhaps she also had had an initiation, a deep look into all she needed to change, a call to self-discipline, to grow up out of the reactiveness of her childhood, and she had resolved to meet it. She let out a long sigh.

"Tired?" Jesse asked. "We just crossed the line into western Massachusetts. Not too much farther now. There's a nice restaurant down the road a bit where I've stopped a number of times. How about some dinner?"

A little later they were seated in a quiet corner of a small, rustic restaurant. Meg felt as if she were in a dream. In front of her was a crisp salad and an elegant plate of food—a lamb chop, new potatoes, and peas. All she could eat. There was a candle lit in the center of the table and across from her Jesse, smiling at her. Just the two of them, no children interrupting and demanding. It felt like the early days of their courtship.

"I want to tell you about my job," he was saying. "It's going to last this time. I talked frankly with the department head—Jim Barrett is his name, a good man—and told him what had happened at my last job. He commended me for speaking up and told me that if there were any racial problems or problems with cheating he wanted to know about it right away. This is a big university in New England, Meg, not a small college in North Carolina. It's going to be okay."

As he talked, Meg felt a forgotten sensation creeping into her body—the sensation of ease. It was as if every fiber in her body had been stretched tight for so long that she had lost the ability to soften. The ease was just a whisper, a soft ripple running through her, a beginning, but with it came hope.

"The University has been generous," Jesse continued. "They're paying for all the expenses of this trip and for our moving expenses, and they're also giving me an advance so we can get settled. Barrett has even set me up with a realtor who will meet with us tomorrow. It's the best salary I've ever had. And I'm really looking forward to teaching again."

Meg reached across the table to squeeze Jesse's hand. "I'm so glad. I hated it when you were working on the road crew, wasting all your gifts and education."

Jesse smiled and returned her squeeze. "Remember, working on the road crew was part of my education."

As they ate, Jesse shared his experiences in Boston, job hunting and tutoring, and Meg shared stories of the children's antics and learnings.

It was another hour and half of driving, now in the dark, before they reached Boston and their hotel room. After a minimum of preparation, they fell, exhausted, into the double bed and slept.

Annie didn't even know she'd been asleep when Aunt Nellie opened the door again. She came and sat on the edge of Annie's bed. "Did you have a little nap? Dinner is almost ready. Let's get you up and change your clothes."

Annie sat up. "My clothes are clean. I just put them on this morning."

"Grandma would like you to wear a dress for dinner. Which one do you want to put on?"

Annie got up from the bed and went to the closet. Her legs weren't shaky anymore. "The blue one."

"Would you like me to help you change?"

"I can do it." Did Aunt Nellie think she was still three? "I've been dressing myself for years."

Aunt Nellie puckered her lips as if she were trying not to smile, but the corners of her eyes crinkled. "That's good," she said. "Comb your hair, too. You look a little tousled. Then come on down. Dinner's almost ready."

The owl scratch hurt when Annie pulled off her shirt. Was it still bleeding? She didn't want to get blood on her blue dress. She went to the mirror on top of the bureau so she could see the scratch. Some of the bandaids had stains on them, but they weren't wet. She noticed that the purple stain on her cheek was almost gone. She put on her blue dress, but she'd forgotten when she told Aunt Nellie she could do it herself, that she didn't know how to tie the sash in the back.

Her hair did look funny. One side of it stuck out and the other side was flat. Was that what tousled meant? She picked up her comb and pulled it through her curls. It didn't help. The side still stuck out.

Annie slammed the comb down on the bureau. Nothing was working. She couldn't tie her sash or make her hair look right. She felt like hitting something. She wanted Mama to be there and fix her hair. She wanted to be home. She didn't want to go downstairs all by herself and have dinner with Grandma and Aunt Nellie. She spun around, went back to her bed and curled up, hugging her pillow.

After a while Aunt Nellie came. "Annie, dinner's ready. It's time for you to come down. What's wrong?"

Annie didn't want to move. But she was hungry. She uncurled and sat up. "I can't tie my sash and my hair won't stop sticking out."

"Oh, dearie, let me help you. Stand up now so I can tie your sash."

After the sash was tied and Aunt Nellie had touched up Annie's hair, they went down to the dining room where Grandma was already sitting at the table. Aunt Nellie bustled around and served their plates—chicken, mashed potatoes and green beans. It smelled so good that Annie picked up her fork and took a big bite of mashed potatoes.

"Wait, Annie," Grandma said. "We haven't said blessing yet."

Annie got that feeling in her tummy again that she'd done something wrong. She put down her fork, but she still had mashed potatoes in her mouth. She held her mouth still.

"Fold your hands like this," Aunt Nellie said. She put her hands together in front of her chest with the fingers pointing up. "And bow your head."

Aunt Nellie and Grandma bowed their heads. Annie put her hands together the way they did and bowed her head, too.

"Dear Lord," Aunt Nellie said, "we thank you that Annie has come to visit us and we thank you for this food. In Jesus name. Amen." She lifted her head. "Now you can eat."

Annie swallowed her mashed potatoes. They were kind of runny from staying in her mouth so long.

"Don't you say blessing at home?" Grandma asked.

Annie didn't know what to say. She knew Grandma wouldn't like it if she said they didn't, but Daddy had told her never to lie.

Aunt Nellie spoke. "Remember, Mama, Jesse's become an agnostic. So I imagine they don't say blessing."

"An agnostic," Grandma muttered. "Dreadful."

Annie didn't know what an agnostic was, but if it was dreadful then Daddy couldn't be it.

Grandma asked her what she had been doing. She didn't want to say she had been in the woods the night before, and she couldn't talk about the kittens. "Mama is teaching me to read," she said. "I can read two books."

Grandma smiled at her then. "That's wonderful. Did you bring your books?"

Annie nodded.

"Then you must read to me tomorrow."

All through dinner Annie tried to have her best manners, to keep one hand in her lap, to say "please" and "thank you," and not talk with her mouth full. When dinner was over, she helped Aunt Nellie clear the table. Then she was tired and went up the big stairs to her room.

Before she even opened the door, she heard a kitten squealing. She hurried in and ran to the basket. Misty was nursing Buttercup, but Dusty had crawled away from his mama and was pushing his nose against the hard wicker side of the basket.

"Oh, Dusty," Annie said to him. "You won't find any milk there." She picked him up and cradled him a moment in her hand. He was so tiny and soft. He had stopped squealing and was now pushing his nose into her palm. Annie laid him down beside Misty. "Here's your mama." Misty lifted her head, gave him a lick, and put her paw over him.

Once she'd seen that Dusty was nursing, Annie went and sat on the windowsill. Dusk was coming and there were pink clouds in the sky. Below her the lawn was turning a soft gray green and the trees were dark against the blue gray sky. There was one tree in the middle of the lawn that Annie especially liked. She remembered it from when she had lived there long ago.

After a while, Misty jumped up beside her. Together they sat looking out as the sky darkened. "All the right and wrong things are different here," Annie told her cat. "I get all mixed up."

She'd lived here a long time when she was three, but then Mama was with her and told her what to do. She remembered now that they used to bow their heads before they ate, but she still didn't know why or who Dear Lord was or why Aunt Nellie was talking to someone who wasn't there. Mama had told her that bowing her head and putting her hands in front of her chest was something about God, but Annie couldn't remember what it was.

She wondered again if the sky was God. She'd have to ask Mama. No. She couldn't. She wasn't going to talk to Mama anymore. How could she not talk to Mama when they were all going to live together in the new house? She tried to remember her mad and how she was going to make Mama sorry, but she didn't feel it anymore. Anyway Daddy had already told Aunt Nellie.

Annie just felt lost, like Dusty getting lost and bumping his nose against the side of the basket.

Aunt Nellie came in. "Are you sitting there all by your lonesome? Come, dearie, it's time to get you into bed."

She helped Annie out of her dress and into her nightgown, and this time Annie didn't say she could do it herself. They went down the hall to the bathroom. Aunt Nellie changed the bandaids on the owl scratch and Annie brushed her teeth and peed. When they got back to Annie's room, Annie started to climb in bed but Aunt Nellie told her to kneel down by the bed first and say her prayers.

Annie just wanted to get in bed. She felt like crying. "I don't know how to say prayers."

Aunt Nellie sighed. "Kneel down with me. I'll say them for you tonight." She held onto the edge the bed to bend her knees and knelt down beside Annie. Annie was so tired she didn't understand what Aunt Nellie said. Lots of God bless and something about Jesus watching over her.

Then Aunt Nellie showed her how to turn the light beside her bed off and on. She turned it off, kissed Annie goodnight and left, closing the door behind her.

Annie leaned over the side of the bed to stroke Buttercup and Dusty in their basket. Misty curled up against her. Annie loved the way Misty's purring jiggled inside her chest.

Night had been going on a long time, when she dreamed. She was back under the spruce tree, looking for the trowel. It was dark, dark. She couldn't see anything. She was crawling on her hands and knees, reaching, groping, but all she could feel was spruce needles. She couldn't find the kittens, or the trowel, or her stick. Right above her she heard the owl hooting.

She woke shaking with fear. Misty was still beside her. The room was dark, but there were two pale squares where the windows were. She leaned over the side of the bed and touched the kittens in their basket. A shuddering sigh shook her. "It's okay," she told Misty. "It was a dream. There's no owl here."

◆§ *Chapter 11* ?◆

When Annie woke the next morning, the sun was shining in the double windows. Misty was sitting on the windowsill looking out, and the kittens were curled together in their basket. Safe.

Annie stretched. She felt better this morning. The room felt familiar. She was remembering more from when they'd lived there when she was three. What you were supposed to do in the morning was get dressed and make your bed and then go downstairs for breakfast. When she was three, Mama had helped her, but she was five now so she did those things herself. Now she also needed to take care of Misty.

She took Misty's water dish with her when she went to the bathroom and brought it back full with fresh water. Then she opened the bottom drawer of the bureau where she had stored the bag of Misty's food and filled her food dish. She sat with Misty a few minutes while Misty ate her breakfast. Then she bent to kiss Misty's head. "I have to go get my breakfast now," she told her kitty. She let herself quietly out the door and shut it behind her.

When she got to the big stairs, she remembered how she and Donny used to slide down the banister. It had been fun but kind of scary when she was three. This time it wasn't scary, just fun, especially when she went around the curve at the bottom. She missed Donny and the way he always yelled "Whee!" when he slid down. Annie didn't yell out loud, but she felt the whee inside.

Aunt Nellie was in the kitchen. When Annie came in, she set down the pan she was holding and came to hug Annie.

"Here you are," she said. "I was about to come up and see if you were awake yet. Are you hungry?"

"Uh huh." Whatever Aunt Nellie was cooking smelled really good.

"How about some blueberry pancakes and scrambled eggs?"

Annie's mouth watered. Pancakes! She hadn't had those for a long time.

Aunt Nellie pulled out a chair at the kitchen table. "Come sit down. Grandma and I have already eaten. After you finish breakfast, Grandma would like you to read to her."

Annie sat down at the table and Aunt Nellie brought her some orange juice and a plate with pancakes and scrambled eggs. There was syrup to go on the pancakes. When Annie cleaned her plate, Aunt Nellie brought her more pancakes. Annie ate until she was so full her tummy was all stretched and tight. Then she took her plate and glass and put it by the sink.

"Thank you," Aunt Nellie said. "You're such a good little girl."

Upstairs in her room, Annie picked up her two books. She went back downstairs, found Grandma in her chair, and read both books to her. Grandma really liked that and told her she was smart to be able to read when she was only five. Then Grandma said she thought she had some other books in the library that were easy to read. She'd ask Aunt Nellie to find them and she'd help Annie to read them. Maybe tomorrow.

As she carried her books back to her room, Annie felt tall. She still missed Daddy and Mama and Donny, but she was okay. She was remembering how to do things here, and Grandma and Aunt Nellie thought she was smart and good. And Uncle Don was going to come soon and take her down to the farm to see some baby goats.

She put on her long pants and combed her hair again. Misty was back on the windowsill. Annie could tell she wanted to go outside, but the screen on the window didn't have a loose corner like the one at home and there was no tree nearby to climb down.

"I'll take you out later," Annie promised. "We can play on that lawn with the big tree, and you can climb it if you want."

Uncle Don came. "Where's my Annie?" he called from the front hall. His voice was like Daddy's. Annie slid down the banister and he plucked her off at the bottom and gave her a big hug.

"Are you ready? Shall we go?"

For the next hour Annie and Uncle Don visited the farm animals—the pigs, the chickens, and the goats. The goats were Annie's favorite because there were two babies. They let Annie pet them, and she loved touching their soft fur and looking into their odd eyes.

Then suddenly she was tired. It was hot and she was thirsty and her legs just didn't want to stand up anymore. She sat down on a bale of straw in the corner of the goat pen. Uncle Don had been talking to a man who helped take care of the goats. When he saw Annie sit down, he said, "It's getting hot, isn't it? Let's go over to the farmhouse now. Mr. and Mrs. Olson remember you and want to see you. You can sit and rest on their nice shady porch. I bet Mrs. Olson would have something cool for you to drink. Would you like that?"

Annie nodded. "I *am* kind of thirsty."

She remembered Mr. and Mrs. Olson. Mrs. Olson always wanted to hold Annie in her lap and Mr. Olson had a big yellow cat. She wondered if the cat she'd seen the day before in front of the farmhouse was the same one.

Uncle Don told Annie that the Olsons were old now and didn't work on the farm anymore, but they could still stay in the farmhouse because their son was taking care of the farm.

Mr. Olson was sitting on the porch swing. When he saw Annie he gave her a big smile. Then he called into the house, "Mary, Annie's here." Mrs. Olson came hurrying out.

"There you are, Annie. You've gotten so big." She bent down and gave Annie a hug and kiss. "You look kind of hot. Would you like some lemonade?"

"Yes. Thank you."

"I'm going to check on some repairs they're doing on the barn," Uncle Don said. "I'll be back for you in a little while."

"Come sit up here with me." Mr. Olson patted the swing beside him. Annie climbed up and Mr. Olson rocked the swing back and forth. The yellow cat was sitting on the railing close beside the swing.

"Is that the same cat you had when I was here before?" Annie asked.

"Sure is. That's my Sunny."

"Because he's yellow like the sun?"

"That's right."

Annie got off the swing and went closer to Sunny. He was much bigger than Misty. He looked strong with lots of muscles. His eyes were yellow like his fur. Annie put out her hand and stroked his back.

"I have a kitty, too," she said. "Her name is Misty 'cause she's gray like mist. And she just had babies."

"I remember Misty," Mr. Olson said. "Your daddy got her for you from the litter of one of our barn cats. She was a pretty little one."

"She still is. She's beautiful."

"And now she's all grown up and having babies?"

"Yes. And one of them is yellow like Sunny. Her name is Buttercup."

Annie thought of the kittens who had died and was sad, but she didn't want to tell Mr. Olson about that.

She was still petting Sunny. His fur wasn't as soft as Misty's. She moved her hand up to scratch behind his ears.

He whipped his head around and bit her finger.

"Ow!" Annie pulled her hand back and put it up to her mouth. Tears stung her eyes.

"Sunny, stop that," Mr. Olson said.

Sunny jumped down off the railing and stalked off into the bushes beside the porch with his tail in the air.

"He bit me," Annie said, her tears spilling over. "Why did he bite me? I wasn't doing anything bad."

Mr. Olson held out his hand. "Here, let me see."

Annie gave him her hand. He turned it over and looked at it carefully. "It was just a nip," he said. "No blood."

"Why did he bite me?" Annie asked again. Her tears were running down her cheeks now. "He's a mean cat."

"No, no." Mr. Olson shook his head. "He's not mean. He's a good cat. He's one of my best friends, follows me around, talks to me, curls up with me when I take a nap. And sometimes he bites. That's just how he is."

Mrs. Olson came out with three tall glasses of lemonade on a tray. When she saw Annie's tears, she asked, "What's wrong, honey?"

"She was petting Sunny and he gave her a nip," Mr. Olson said. "She's okay, aren't you Annie? I think he hurt your feelings more than your finger."

Annie's finger didn't hurt anymore. Mr. Olson was right. She smiled at him and rubbed the tears off her cheeks with the back of her hand. "Yeah. I wanted him to like me."

"He will. He just needs to get to know you. He's a good cat, like I said. Now come here and sit beside me and have some lemonade."

Annie climbed back on the swing beside Mr. Olson. Mrs. Olson gave them each a glass of lemonade and settled herself in a rocker nearby.

The lemonade was cold and tasted really good. Mr. Olson put his arm around Annie and that felt good, too. He and Mrs. Olson asked her about Misty and she had fun telling them all the things Misty could do.

After a while, Uncle Don came back and he and Annie walked back to Grandma's house. All the way up the hill, Annie thought about Sunny.

Chapter Eleven ≈ 163

Meg woke to the low whir of a fan, and the dim, cool hotel room, the windows shaded by dark blue curtains. Jesse was curled around her, his body cradling hers, his kisses on her neck and hair. She turned into his arms and they made love, long, deep, and sweet. Afterward she lay with her head on his shoulder, soaking in the feel of him, drinking in the reassurance of his love.

She turned her head into his chest. "I love you so much," she whispered.

He tightened his arms around her.

"You know," Meg said, wanting to confess, daring to ask for still more assurance, "That terrible night when Annie was in the woods, I was so afraid, so ashamed of what I had done, I thought maybe you would leave me and take the children away from me because I was such a bad mother."

"*What?*" Jesse leaned up on his elbow and looked down into her face. "I would never leave you. You're my wife. I'm promised to you for life. And you're not a bad mother. What nonsense is that? Yes, you have a problem with your temper, but that is only a tiny part of you. You're a good mother. You give the children such fine attention, play with them, teach them."

Meg started to speak. "It's just that —"

But Jesse interrupted her. "Why would I leave you. I *love* you. I love your brilliant mind, your humor, your affectionate ways. I continue to marvel at the way you take on new challenges and do well with them. I love talking with you, making music with you. These last months have been bleak without you."

Meg stilled her breath in astonishment. Jesse had always been affectionate, but he was reserved. She didn't remember ever hearing such an outburst from him. She felt as if a flower were opening in her heart. He did love her. He saw the best of her. Tears slipped from her eyes.

Jesse wiped them away with his gentle hand. "What is it?"

"For months now I've been feeling like nothing more than an ill-tempered drudge. You just reminded me of the other parts of myself."

He lay down again and gathered her close. "I'm so sorry you've had such a hard time, that I didn't check in with you more often or have any idea what you were going through. I'm going to be with you now, and if bumps come along, we'll ride them together."

They lay quiet in each other's arms. Meg felt herself softening, easing, remembering who she was. Not just a drudge. A woman loved.

After a while, Jesse stirred. "How about some breakfast, and then an expedition to find our new home?"

Meg didn't even have to fix breakfast. They just went downstairs to the hotel dining room and were waited on. She still hadn't gotten used to having as much as she wanted to eat. She'd been holding back so long so there would be more for the children. This ample breakfast felt like luxury indeed. Maybe, she thought, part of her quick temper and headaches was because she had been chronically hungry. As she took the last bite of her cinnamon roll, she realized she felt better than she'd felt in a long time.

Jesse went to the pay phone in the lobby and called Ruth the realtor. Half an hour later, Ruth met them in the lobby of the hotel. She was tall with stylishly cut dark hair and such a strong Boston accent that, throughout the day, Meg struggled at times to keep a straight face.

They looked at three houses in the city near the University. They were all okay houses, certainly better than the one in Woodsborough, but Meg was uncomfortable with the ambiance of city noise and concerned about the amount of traffic on the streets.

"I wouldn't want Donny riding his bike here," she said. "And Misty wouldn't be safe with all these cars going by so fast."

"I have a house for rent with an option to buy out in Melrose," Ruth said. "Melrose is a nice suburb about a twenty minute drive from the University with good schools, a library, shops of all kinds. The house is in a quiet neighborhood on a street only two blocks long."

A library! Meg thought. How wonderful it would be to go to the library, find books to read, books for the children.

"Let's have a look at it," Jesse said. "If it's a good place, I wouldn't mind a short commute."

They stopped for lunch, then drove to Melrose, to a neighborhood of large, comfortable-looking houses, mature trees, and wide, well-kept lawns. Children played kickball in the street. They ran aside to let the car pass, then resumed their play.

The tall Victorian house was at the end of the street. Two poplar trees framed the front walk. On both the first and second floors there were big bay windows, and a screened-in porch stretched across the front of the house.

The front door opened into a hall and a wide, winding staircase. Downstairs there was a kitchen with a pantry almost as big as the whole kitchen in Woodsborough, a dining room, and a living room. Upstairs, three bedrooms, a den for Jesse, and a bathroom. The big front bedroom with its own bay window would be a perfect love bower for her and Jesse. There was even a third floor with a partly finished attic.

As they walked through the house, Meg felt her excitement grow. She paused in the upstairs hall, looking into the bedrooms that would be for the children. It would be good for them to each have their own room. Donny would welcome the space and the independence, she knew. And Annie … maybe … maybe she could win Annie back by engaging her in the project of decorating her room. Meg imagined pink ruffled curtains and a matching bedspread. She smiled inwardly as she remembered Annie telling her that pink was Misty's favorite color.

When they went back downstairs, Meg started planning where everything would go. All the rooms were spacious with big windows, and plenty of room to hold all the furniture stored at Mama and Nellie's as well as everything crowded into their Woodsborough home.

Meg especially loved the living room with the bay window. She visualized their big upholstered chair in its curve, with a table beside it piled with library books. There was lots of space for all their bookcases, the Victrola, and her good couch. She imagined herself sitting there with the children snuggled up on either side as she read to them. Then felt a chill. Would Annie ever cuddle up to her again? For a moment, all her excitement about the house was submerged by the piercing ache to hold her little girl in her arms again.

Jesse touched her shoulder. "Come see. There's a screened-in back porch, too."

Meg startled back to the present moment and followed Jesse and Ruth out the kitchen door. Steps from the back porch led down into a small lawn surrounded by flower beds and enclosed by a white picket fence with an arch over the gate covered with late blooming roses. It was all perfect. Meg's excitement returned. She turned to Jesse. "What do you think?"

"I think this house would do very well."

"Are you okay with the commute?"

"To live here, yes. What about you?"

"I love it. Can we take it?"

Jesse was grinning widely. "We sure can."

Ruth was smiling, too. "Then let's go see the landlord. He lives just across town."

The landlord was home, and within a half hour, they had a contract and keys to the house. Ruth took them back to their hotel. As they passed through the lobby, the attendant called them over. They had a message.

Jesse opened it. "It's an invitation from Jim Barrett, the chair of my department, the man I told you about. We are invited to dinner at his home this evening." Jesse turned the message in his hands. "I was thinking we'd check out, head home, and start packing, but maybe we should do this. It's a gracious invitation. I'd like to have you meet Jim and his wife. The University gave us three hotel nights and we've only used one. What do you think?"

Meg felt torn. She wanted to get back to the children, but the thought of a dinner with Jesse's new colleague and another night in the luxury of the hotel was tempting. "I guess the children will be all right another night without us. I'd like to."

"Good." Jesse smiled at her. "The children will be fine. Donny seemed quite at home and welcome at Jack's house, and Nellie will take good care of Annie. It might even be good for you and Annie to have a little longer break from each other."

His last words jolted Meg, but maybe he was right.

"Okay, let's accept," she said. Concerns about Annie shifted to a thrill of excitement at the thought of making her first social connection in the university community, of dining with an educated couple. She was glad she had brought her good yellow dress and heels.

Jesse went to the pay phone in the lobby and called to accept the invitation.

It was only four o'clock when they got back to their room, and their dinner wasn't until six. Jesse took Meg in his arms.

"Let's have a nap."

Aunt Nellie told Annie that she and Grandma took a nap after lunch and suggested that Annie nap, too.

So Annie lay down on her bed, but she wasn't sleepy. After a while, she got up and took Misty's ball out of the top drawer of the bureau. She rolled it across the room and Misty chased it and batted it back to her. Usually Misty really liked that game, but after only a little while, she stopped batting the ball back and jumped up on the windowsill. She swished her tail, looked straight at Annie and meowed. Her message was clear. She wanted to go outside.

Annie wanted to go out, too. She wanted to lie on the grass and look at the tree against the sky. "We can go, Misty," she told her cat.

"We just need to be really quiet so we don't wake up Grandma and Aunt Nellie."

Annie checked on Dusty and Buttercup in their basket. They were sleeping, curled up together. They would be fine for a little while.

When Aunt Nellie had taken Annie to the garden to get dirt for the litter box, they'd gone down a back stairway and out a back door that opened into the garden and, beyond that, the big lawn. Annie decided to go that way. She picked Misty up, slipped out of her room and closed the door behind her.

She knew how to be quiet and Misty seemed to understand she needed to be quiet, too. Annie tiptoed down the hall past the open door of Aunt Nellie's room. Aunt Nellie lay stretched out on her bed with her mouth open, fast asleep. Without a sound, Annie went on to the back of the house, softly down the back stairs, and out the back door. Misty wiggled to get down, and Annie followed her as she scampered along the garden path and out onto the big lawn.

It was a really nice lawn, green and thick and soft, not like the hard, prickly lawn at home. Annie sat down and put her hands in the grass. It was so smooth and soft that she took off her shoes and socks.

Misty had run ahead of her and was already halfway up the big tree, perched where two branches separated. She peered down at Annie, then whisked her tail and ran up higher. Annie laughed. She loved seeing Misty climb; she was so quick and frisky.

The tree called to her, too. She went to the trunk and leaned against it. This tree felt different from her spruce tree, but it also was gentle and peaceful. Annie slid her hands down the trunk, lay on the soft grass underneath, and looked up into the tree.

The deep green leaves were shaped like little hands with lots of fingers, and moved slightly in the breeze. Beyond the leaves, the sky. It was right up against the leaves and far, far away, so far Annie couldn't see the end of it. How could there be something that had no end? How could the sky be so close to the tree and so far away? But Mama had said they were both true. Between the tree and the faraway sky, there were white puffy clouds which only made the sky look farther away. Then Annie felt the sky all around her, touching her. It was even inside her; she was breathing the sky and sinking into the grass. Her body ached with a good ache.

She started thinking of Mama. Daddy had asked her in the car to tell him about gentle Mama. She didn't want to then because she was still mad. But now she wasn't mad anymore and she missed gentle Mama. Mama was teaching her to read. Grandma said she was lucky to have a mama who would do that. Mama taught her songs and sang with her. Mama helped her learn to do things like tying her shoes. Maybe she could teach Annie how to tie her sash in back. Gentle Mama helped her make things like the garden in the glass dish. She read a story to Annie and Donny every night and said the "Night" poem to Annie when she tucked her in.

The "Night" poem always made Annie feel safe and peaceful. She knew all the words and could say it to herself, but it was much better when she and Mama said it together.

A scrabbling sound interrupted her thoughts. Misty was coming down the tree backwards. Just before she reached the bottom, she jumped off and came to Annie. She settled in the grass, licked her paw, wrapped it around her ear, and began washing herself.

Annie lay quietly watching her and thinking more about Mama. Maybe she was like Sunny, a gentle Mama most of the time, but sometimes she hit. That was just how she was. Annie sat up to think about that more.

"Maybe we don't need to be scared of Mama anymore," she told Misty. "She promised not to hurt Dusty and Buttercup and if she starts to hit me, I can dodge. Like this."

She jumped up and darted sideways the way Donny had showed her. "And like this." She ducked to the other side, then dropped to the ground and rolled. It was fun. She dodged and rolled several more times. "Then you've got to run, really fast." She tore across the lawn. Misty raced after her. The next time she dropped to the ground, Misty jumped right over her and pounced on her ankle. Annie rolled on her back, breathless and laughing.

Of course, Donny had said that the best thing to do was to get far away as soon as she saw Mama getting mad. Annie knew what Mama looked like when she was getting mad. She got all swelled up, and her eyes pushed out. She looked the way Annie had felt when she was mad at Mama.

Annie went suddenly still. She remembered when she was mad that she'd wanted to hit Mama. And kick her. No! She didn't want to become like witch Mama. She didn't want to hit or hurt anyone. She must never ever get mad again.

She rolled over and curled onto her side. She hadn't kicked Mama, but she'd been mean. She knew Mama was sad when Annie wouldn't let Mama touch her. She should give Mama a hug when she and Daddy came.

Chapter 12

The second day Annie was at Grandma's house, Aunt Nellie found two books in the library for Annie to practice reading. They had lots of pictures and there were many words that Annie already knew. She spent a long time with Grandma learning new words and reading the new stories. Annie really liked that, and Grandma said she did, too. Aunt Nellie told her the books had belonged to her daddy when he was learning to read and that she could keep them. After lunch, Annie took them up to her room, hugging them against her chest. New treasures. She sat on her bed, looking through them again, remembering the stories and touching the new words she had learned.

But after a while she wanted to go outside. Misty did, too. All the while Annie had been looking at her books, Misty had been sitting on the windowsill looking out, swishing her tail.

Grandma and Aunt Nellie were still napping. They took really long naps. Annie picked up Misty and they went the way they had gone the day before, down the hall to the back stairs and out through the garden. As soon as Annie put her down, Misty raced for the big tree.

Annie followed more slowly. Aunt Nellie had told her at lunch that Daddy had called. He and Mama had found a house in Boston and now they were back in Woodsborough and would come at suppertime today to visit Grandma and pick up Annie. They were going to spend the night. Annie's thoughts were all bunched up in her head and her heart felt trembly.

She leaned against the trunk of the big tree. Even though she knew she could dodge, she felt scared again. Mama was so big and strong. Maybe Annie wouldn't be quick enough. Maybe Mama would hit her hard and make her cheek all purple again. Even if Annie did her very best not to do wrong things, Mama might still get mad at her.

Mama said she wouldn't hurt Dusty and Buttercup. But what if Buttercup, when she got bigger, knocked something off a shelf and broke it? Or what if Dusty peed on the rug. Mama might get so mad she'd hit them before she remembered her promise.

Mama wasn't really like Sunny. When Sunny bit, it was just a nip; it didn't even break the skin. But when Mama hit, she made Annie's cheek purple. If Mama hit Dusty or Buttercup that hard it would kill them, and then Annie and Misty would have no kittens left.

Annie slid slowly down the trunk of the tree until she was sitting on the grass underneath. She suddenly felt like crying.

She wanted her gentle Mama so much. She wanted gentle Mama to hold her and love her and always be gentle. But gentle Mama was all twisted up with witch Mama. Annie would never know when the witch would come out.

She felt a big ache like a deep black hole in the center of her chest, an ache that hurt way worse even than the owl scratch. Daddy said the owl scratch would stop hurting after a while. He said it was deep, but not so bad it needed stitches. He fixed it with iodine and bandaids. But how could anyone fix the ache inside her? Maybe it would never get well.

Could stitches close up a hole? Maybe.

Even though Annie knew pretend things weren't really real, she couldn't help pretending again.

She lay down in the grass, looked up into the tree, and pretended a magic elf doctor came to sew up the hole in her heart. Because he was magic, it wouldn't even hurt. The elf doctor was little, littler than her new doll, dressed in a green suit and a pointed green hat. He had a curly brown beard, and wise, kind eyes. His magic needle was golden and the thread silver, but the hole was so deep he couldn't sew it together. Annie tried really hard to pretend he could, but he just couldn't.

"Never mind," he told her. "I can sew up the outside so no one will know the hole is there." She imagined him working back and forth across her chest, pulling the skin together until it was all smooth. That made Annie feel a little better. No one would know, and maybe she could forget about it after a while.

But she also knew it was only pretend, like making up the elves' magic castle in the woods. The elves never really came.

Daddy came.

Daddy had said Mama wouldn't hit her anymore. He would make sure of it. Maybe it would be safe if Daddy were there. And Mama was gentle most of the time. Annie remembered all the gentle things about Mama that she had thought of the day before.

She let out a long shuddering sigh. Daddy would be there. Maybe it would be okay. And she missed Mama. She wanted Mama to hold her in her lap, tuck her in at night. She wanted to show Mama her new books and the new words she'd learned with Grandma. Mama would be proud of her. She wanted Mama to say the "Night" poem with her.

Annie remembered that she had promised herself never to get mad again, so she wouldn't be like witch Mama. She'd decided she wouldn't be mean to Mama. She would talk to Mama again and let Mama touch her. She'd planned to give Mama a hug when she came.

But now she was really coming. Today.

Annie lay stiff in the grass. The scared feeling was all over her body. She felt sick in her tummy.

High up in the tree Misty peered down at her.

"Kitty, kitty," Annie called to her.

Misty descended so fast, jumping from one branch to the one below, that Annie caught her breath. But Misty never fell. She was a really good climber. A moment later, she was beside Annie. Annie scooped her up and hugged her kitty against her chest. The warmth of her eased the pain in Annie's heart.

"Mama's coming," Annie told her. "Daddy said we have to get along. So I have to be nice and let her touch me and talk to her. But we've got to watch out, cause we'll never know when she'll turn into a witch again, and we'll have to duck or run and hide the kittens."

Aunt Nellie came to the back door. "Annie," she called. "Your mama and daddy will be here soon. Come on in now. Let's give you a bath and put on one of your pretty dresses."

◆ ◆

The last kitchen box done. Meg taped it up, marked it, and set it on top of the pile. All that was left was food in the refrigerator which they would pack in their ice box tomorrow and take with them.

She was hot, sweaty, and tired, but happy. It had been a long day, but a good one. They'd gotten up early to get out of Boston before the morning traffic, stopped in Worchester for breakfast and to pick up packing materials and a crate for Misty and the kittens to travel in.

"It would be unlikely to find this stuff in Woodsborough," Jesse had said. "The crate is important. Misty was uncomfortable driving over to Mama's. She usually sticks close to Annie, but I'm afraid she might get frightened and bolt when we stop along the way. This will keep her safe."

Meg was grateful that Jesse had thought of those things. Relief coursed through her as she realized anew that it wasn't all up to her anymore.

They'd reached Woodsborough just before the noon whistle blew, eaten a quick lunch from leftovers, and set to work. They started in the living room and sang folk songs and rounds together as they packed books and records. With two of them working, it had gone quickly and actually been fun. Then Jesse had gone upstairs and Meg into the kitchen. As she'd packed the dishes, she'd heard him still singing, his sweet, clear tenor.

Meg was checking the cupboards and pantry one last time when Jesse stuck his head in the kitchen door. "The children's room is done. There's still our room and the bathroom, to say nothing of the shed and basement, but we can get those tomorrow. Let's clean up and get ready now. Nellie will get anxious if we're late."

Half an hour later they were on the road again. Meg settled into the car seat and leaned her head back. They'd been working so hard that she hadn't thought about Annie all day. When she'd had time to think, it had been about their new house and the evening with the Barretts. That had gone well. They were lovely people and Meg knew she had made a good impression.

Now, as they drove toward the farm, Meg's fears about Annie loomed. What if Annie still wouldn't speak to her or let Meg touch her? What if Annie never forgave her? What if Meg's relationship to her precious little girl had been shattered the way the windshield would be if a stone hit it?

The late afternoon sun shone in the side window and poured over Meg's lap and arm. She stifled a moan and shifted in her seat.

Jesse laid his hand on her thigh. "How are you doing?"

"Getting a little anxious," Meg confessed.

"About seeing Annie again?"

"Yes. I don't know what I can do if she still won't talk to me."

"Annie called you 'gentle Mama' when she was telling me about the times she felt you loved her. I'd say be your best gentle mama. I think she'll come to you. I'm guessing she's been missing you."

"I hope so."

There was more Meg needed to say, about the promise Jesse had asked for: never to strike the children again. In spite of her resolution to make the promise to Jesse, she hadn't in all the time they'd been together the last two days. It was such an important promise to make, so important that she never break it.

She started to speak, but lost her nerve and went off on a tangent. "Mama's going to be disappointed not to see Donny," she said.

"She will," Jesse agreed. He put his hand back on the wheel. "But this last night with Jack is important to him. He's growing up fast, turning more of his focus out from the nest."

Yes, Meg thought, it was obvious. When they'd stopped at the Martins as they came into Woodsborough, Donny didn't want to go with them. He'd come and given them each a quick hug and then run off with Jack. Ada explained that on Mike's day off, he and the boys had finished the tree house and Jack and Donny were planning to sleep in it that night. An adventure that could hardly be denied just to visit a grandmother.

"Are you sure it's all right with you to have him another night?" Meg had asked Ada.

"Oh, yes! Jack's had such a good time with Donny." Tears suddenly came to Ada's round blue eyes. "You know, I always wanted lotsa kids, but I had trouble having Jack and then couldn't have any more. We love having Donny here. Wish we could keep him."

So they'd left him for one more night. Remembering the tears in Ada's eyes, Meg felt a rush of compassion for her and realized how lucky she was to have her two beautiful children.

Which brought her back to Annie. She saw again the purple stain on Annie's cheek. She'd never meant to hit her that day she'd stayed up in the woods all morning. All Annie had needed was a reprimand for staying away so long.

The promise solidified in her. She *would* control herself. And maybe if she never hit Annie again, Annie would forgive her and love and trust her as she used to.

Chapter Twelve 🙰 177

Meg turned in her seat and looked out the window. She'd have to speak soon if she were going to. She knew the landmarks. They were nearing the farm.

She took in a deep breath and blurted, "You asked me to promise I'd never hit the children again. I've been scared to promise because if I lost control and hit one of them …then … If I broke the promise then you'd never trust me again. But I must promise.

"When I was going upstairs to check on them packing their suitcases I saw Donny teaching Annie to duck. That was terrible. Like they're *expecting* my blows and preparing. It has to end. Like you said. So … I promise you I won't strike our children ever again."

Jesse turned onto the road to the farm, pulled over, and stopped the car. He shifted to face Meg and let out his breath slowly.

"I'm so glad for your promise."

"It's not about punishing them. They're rarely naughty. It's a bad habit, from how I grew up. Striking out when I'm upset. It *has* been a hard time this last year."

Jesse reached out and stroked Meg's cheek. "I know. I want to make it easier for you. I can do more with the children and housework. And I want to find a good babysitter, so we can get away once in a while, just us. I really enjoyed our last two nights."

He laid his hands on her shoulders, then slid them down her arms to hold her hands. "Breaking a long habit is a challenge, but you can do it, Meg. You're a strong woman and have already overcome many obstacles. And I will help. Come to me if you feel the tension rising. We'll tackle this together. Okay?" He looked into her eyes and smiled his loving smile.

Meg smiled back at him through sudden tears. "Okay."

Jesse started the car again and drove down the road toward the farm and Annie.

🙰

Annie sat on the porch of the big house with Aunt Nellie, waiting for Daddy and Mama.

Her tummy was tight and the longer she waited the more the tightness spread all through her. She wanted Daddy and Mama to come really badly, but she was scared again. Would Mama be jagged? How could Annie dare to hug her if she were?

But Daddy would be there. And Aunt Nellie. Mama wouldn't do anything bad with them watching. Annie got up from her chair and went to the porch railing. She wished she could just go down the steps and around the house and run and roll with Misty on the big lawn. But Misty was upstairs in her room and Annie was all cleaned up, wearing her pink-flowered dress. Aunt Nellie had combed her hair a special way and told her not to tousle it.

Annie held tight to the railing and looked down the road. She heard the sound of a car.

Aunt Nellie got up and stood beside Annie. "Here they come."

Then Annie could see Daddy's black car coming around the bend and up the road. It stopped just below the steps, and Daddy got out.

Annie held her breath and squeezed the railing so hard her hands hurt. Mama got out of the other side of the car.

Daddy looked up at her. "Annie," he called. She ran to him then. He caught her as she jumped off the bottom step and picked her up in his arms.

Daddy. He *had* come back. He held her close. She wrapped her arms tight around his neck and pressed her face against his shoulder. He caressed her head, kissed her cheek. Then he said, "Mama's here."

Annie turned her face out of Daddy's shoulder. Mama was standing beside him.

She looked better. There were no dark smudges under her eyes and she was wearing a pretty dress. She wasn't jagged at all. She was looking at Annie with soft brown eyes, like the eyes of the mama deer in the clearing. Her eyes were so gentle. Maybe Mama really did love her.

Her heart opened. "Hi, Mama," she whispered. She held out her hand to Mama and Daddy tipped her right into Mama's arms.

Mama holding her. Mama's smell. Mama kissing her. Mama laying her cheek against Annie's. "I'm so glad to see you," she said.

Annie softened. It felt so good to have Mama hold her and be gentle. She rested her head against Mama's shoulder and, just for a moment, felt safe. Then the image of Mama standing over the rain barrel flashed behind her eyes. She tensed and wiggled to get down. Mama set her down and took her hand.

Aunt Nellie was hugging Daddy and talking. She came up to Mama. "Welcome, Margaret. Come on in now. Dinner's almost ready. Bring your bags. I'll show you your room and you can freshen up."

Daddy took a little suitcase and a wire cage out of the car. Mama kept hold of Annie's hand and they followed Aunt Nellie into the house. Annie's legs felt shaky and she had to hold her breath to keep from crying.

Aunt Nellie took them to the room next to Annie's. "Here you are," she said. "Get settled and then come on down." She hurried off.

"I need to go move the car," Daddy said. "I'll be right back."

Mama sat down suddenly on the bed. She still held Annie's hand. Annie felt scared with Daddy gone, but Mama was looking at her with the love look in her eyes and, in spite of her fear, Annie wanted Mama to hold her more. She leaned against Mama's side and Mama put an arm around her. Then Annie couldn't help it. She started to cry.

Mama gathered Annie into her lap. "What is it, honey?"

"I'm sorry I was mean to you."

Mama tightened her arms around Annie. "Oh, honey. I've been mean to you, too, and I'm terribly sorry. Can we let it go now, forgive each other, and be friends?"

Annie nodded into Mama's shoulder.

They sat there hugging for a while, not saying anything. Annie felt safe one moment and scared the next, but she made herself stay in Mama's lap. She'd stopped crying, but her nose was sniffy.

Mama took a handkerchief out of her pocket and wiped Annie's nose and cheeks. "Okay, now?"

Annie nodded again.

Daddy came back. "It's time to go downstairs. Aunt Nellie and Grandma are waiting for us."

Mama set Annie down. As they walked down the hall, Annie took Daddy's hand. "You have to remember not to eat till they say blessing," she told him.

Daddy looked down at her with a funny smile on his face. "That's right. Thanks for reminding me."

"The first night I was here, I didn't know," Annie explained. "I took a big bite of mashed potatoes before Grandma told me, and I had to hold them in my mouth all the time Aunt Nellie said blessing." It was suddenly funny. Annie giggled and Mama and Daddy laughed out loud.

"They got all squishy before I could swallow them." Daddy and Mama laughed more. Annie loved making them laugh.

Grandma was in the dining room all settled in her chair, and Aunt Nellie brought in dinner—pork chops and baked potatoes and green beans, all from the farm. It was really good. Annie ate until her tummy felt stretched. She was still amazed that she could ask for second helpings.

After dinner, Mama helped Aunt Nellie clean up and then they all sat on the front porch. The grown-ups talked. Annie sat on Daddy's lap and then on Mama's. Mama was being gentle, but Annie felt kind of stiff. After a while Grandma was tired and went to bed.

After she left, Aunt Nellie said, "She's going to miss Annie. You wouldn't believe how much she's brightened up since Annie's been here. I'll miss her, too."

"Grandma's helping me read," Annie told Mama and Daddy. "And I have two new books and I know lots of new words."

"That's wonderful," Mama said. "Will you show me your new books?"

"They're upstairs in my room."

Chapter Twelve 181

"Then let's go on up. It's getting time for you to go to bed, too."

"I'll come with you," Daddy said. "I want to show Misty her new riding basket."

As they climbed the stairs together, Annie asked. "What's Misty's new riding basket? Is it that wire cage you brought in?"

"I'll show you," Daddy said. "Let's put it in your room tonight and put the kittens in it so Misty can get used to it before we travel tomorrow."

Annie was doubtful. "Misty won't like a cage."

"No," Daddy said, "She probably won't. But remember how she was ready to run away when we first got here, and you had to grab her quickly? This will keep her safe when we stop the car to pee or have a picnic. We'll only close the door when we are ready to stop."

When they got upstairs, Daddy brought the cage to Annie's room and set it on the floor beside the kittens' basket. "See," Daddy said. "It has a nice cushion in the bottom. We can put their towel in to make it even softer."

Annie sat down on the floor beside the cage. She reached inside and touched the cushion. It was nice and soft.

"Let's put the kittens inside and leave the door open and let Misty check it out," Daddy said. "I need to go down now and say goodnight to Grandma and talk with Aunt Nellie a little. Mama will help you get settled." He picked Annie up and gave her a kiss, then left.

Annie was alone with Mama again. A quiver of fear ran through her. Mama was sitting on the bed. Annie looked up at her. She still looked gentle.

"Would you like me to help you move the kittens," she asked.

Annie got another fear shiver. "No. I can do it. They're used to me." Carefully, she gathered up the two kittens and set them in her lap. She took the green towel out of the basket and spread it out in the cage.

She looked up at Mama again. Mama still looked gentle but really sad.

Annie knew Mama wanted to hold the kittens. She didn't want Mama to touch them, but she had promised herself to not be mean to Mama.

"You can touch the kittens if you want," Annie said. "Just with the tip of your finger. They're very soft."

Mama smiled then. "I'd love to touch them."

Annie held the kittens up and Mama stroked their heads very gently with the tip of her finger the way she'd taught Annie to do when the kittens were newborn. Then Annie laid the kittens on the green towel in the cage.

Mama wiped a tear off her cheek. "Thank you for letting me touch them. They *are* soft."

"You promised you wouldn't hurt them."

"Yes, I did. I won't hurt them." Mama took a catchy breath. "They're growing. Misty must be feeding them well."

"Yes. They're crawling more now. Last night Dusty got way over on the side of the basket and was crying because he couldn't find his mama."

Misty had been sleeping on the bed. When Annie started moving the kittens, she sat up and watched. Once the kittens were settled, she jumped down and came to examine the cage. She walked around it, sniffed it, tapped the wire side with her paw, then went in through the door and sniffed the kittens. She came out again and looked up at Annie with an inquiring meow.

Annie picked her up. "It's okay, Misty. This is your traveling basket and will keep you and your babies safe until we get to our new home."

Misty wiggled free and went back into the cage to lick her babies.

"Bed time now," Mama said.

She helped Annie out of her dress and into her nightgown. They went to the bathroom for Annie to pee and brush her teeth. Mama wanted to look at the owl scratch, but Annie told her she'd had a bath just before supper and Aunt Nellie had put new bandaids on it. "It's not infected and doesn't hurt so much anymore," Annie told her.

When they got back to Annie's room, Annie showed Mama her new books. They sat on the bed together leaning back against the pillow and the headboard, and Annie read one of the stories to Mama. It felt good reading together again, only sort of funny because Annie was reading instead of Mama. Mama said she was reading very well and she was proud of Annie for learning so many new words.

When they had finished reading and Annie was tucked in bed, she asked, "Will you say the 'Night' poem with me?"

"Yes." Mama sat beside her and they said the words of the poem together.

"The sun descending in the west,

The evening star does shine …"

Annie loved the part when the angels came:

"If they see any weeping

That should have been sleeping

They pour sleep on their head

And sit down by their bed." —

When they finished the poem, Annie pretended to be asleep. Mama bent and kissed her and slipped out of the room.

Annie listened to her mama's footsteps moving away from her down the hall. The ache in her chest rose up again and hurt so much she could hardly breathe. She remembered Mama touching the kittens, and her body went stiff with fear. What if Mama had just squeezed their necks so fast Annie couldn't stop her? The times she'd felt safe in Mama's arms were the worst because she wasn't really safe and might forget to watch out. With a soft moan, she turned on her side and curled up into a ball. No angels came. It was a long time before she fell asleep.

Chapter 13

They were home. Annie went out in the back yard and looked up the path toward the fort. She suddenly realized that they were really leaving, and if she didn't go up into the woods, she'd never see her cave again, or the clearing where the deer were. She'd never be able to lean against the trunk of the spruce tree, or stand on the cliff and look way down, or put new flowers on the kittens' grave. She really wanted to do those things one last time before they left. And it was important to her to bring back the trowel. Every time she thought of how she'd left it up there, she got that bad feeling in her tummy.

She went into the house. Everything felt different. Up in her room, there were no pillows or covers on the beds and Annie's clothes and toys were gone from the closet and the bureau. Mama was in the bathroom packing. She told Annie that all her things were safe in the boxes piled on the bed.

Annie stood outside the bathroom door watching Mama. "I have to go to my cave," she said. "I left the trowel up there."

Mama was busy packing. "No," she said. "The moving truck will be here soon and once they've loaded the furniture and boxes, we'll be on our way. I want you and Donny to stay right here. We can leave the trowel."

"Donny went up to the fort. Daddy told him he could. I need to go."

"Annie, I said no." Mama didn't even look at Annie. She had a frown on her forehead and just kept putting things in a box.

Annie lifted her chin. She felt hot mad rising in her body. "That's not fair. Donny gets to go to his fort."

"I can't have you disappearing into the woods again," Mama said. "We're going to leave soon. What if you get lost?"

"I won't get lost," Annie insisted. "I know the way." Tears were pushing against the back of her eyes, but she still held her chin up. The hot mad was spreading. "Mama, I need to go."

Mama stopped putting things in the box and turned to look at her. "Why is it so important to you?"

"Because we are going away and I won't ever never get a chance to see my cave and my tree again. And put flowers on the kittens' grave." Some of her tears got away from her and started running down her cheeks.

Mama looked softer. "You made a grave for the kittens up there?"

"Yes. Under my tree."

"I see. But you don't have any long pants. Your overalls are dirty and your slacks are too short and expose your ankles."

"The laundry bag is on Donny's bed. I could get my overalls out. They're not too dirty." Annie wouldn't tell Mama she'd peed on them.

Mama put down the box she was packing and turned all the way to look at Annie. "Well … I guess you could go. But you must just get the trowel and come right back, lickety split. Don't linger."

Annie felt a sob rising in her chest. "I don't want to go fast. I want to look at things … " She pushed down her sob. "I could come back when the lunch time whistle blows. I can hear it up there."

Mama's eyes were beginning to push forward. "That won't do. I need you to *be* here at lunch time, not just starting back."

Mama was getting jagged. Annie stepped back. She began to feel hot mad pushing her own eyes forward. "I can come down very fast when I hear the whistle."

Mama set her hands on her hips. "Annie, you either go quickly or not at all. Now leave me alone. Can't you see I'm busy? I have to get all this sorted and packed before the truck comes."

Annie's hot mad pulsed all through her body. "I won't bother you if I'm in the woods."

Mama took her hands off her hips and jerked them out to her sides. "All *right*. Go, then," she said. "But be back as soon as you can."

For a moment, to Annie's surprise, Mama looked scared. "Be careful," she added, and then turned back to the box she was packing.

Swiftly, before Mama changed her mind, Annie dashed into the bedroom and shut the door. She pulled the laundry bag off Donny's bed and rummaged in it until she found her overalls. They had dirt smudges on them and smelled a little like pee, but Annie didn't care. She shed her sun suit and pulled on the overalls. Mama's back was turned when she passed the bathroom. Without making a sound, Annie ran down the stairs.

She stopped in the kitchen. She found she was shaking all over and her heart was beating hard. She had a sick feeling in her tummy. She'd gotten mad at Mama after promising herself she never would again. If she couldn't stop herself being mad, she would end up like witch mama.

Daddy was in the shed pulling things out into back yard. He turned when Annie came through the kitchen door. "What are you up to?"

"I'm going up to see my cave, and put flowers on the kittens' grave, and bring back the trowel I left up there."

"Does Mama know?"

"Yes. At first she said I couldn't go, but we argued, and then she said I could.

The sick feeling in her tummy felt so awful that Annie started crying.

"What's wrong?" Daddy asked.

"I got mad at Mama when she said I couldn't go."

"I can understand that."

"But I promised I'd never ever get mad again."

"Who did you promise?"

"Me."

Daddy sat down on the ground and took Annie in his lap. "Annie, it's okay to get angry. Everybody does sometimes. There are lots of ways to handle anger. It doesn't have to be a bad thing."

"I wanted to kick Mama."

"But you didn't, did you?

"No."

"It sounds like you did very well. You used your anger to stand up for what you wanted and you persuaded Mama to change her mind."

Annie felt very quiet inside. She *had* made Mama change her mind.

"Oh." The quiet feeling inside Annie spread into a feeling of warmth all over her. Not hot mad, but warm. Like she was strong. She sighed a big sigh, and the sick feeling was gone. You could be mad without doing mean things. She was glad she hadn't kicked Mama.

"I have to go now," she said. "Only Mama said I had to come right back as soon as I got the trowel, but I don't want to rush." Tears arose again. "I want to sit in my cave and lean against my tree. She said I had to be back by the noon whistle, but I don't know when the noon whistle will blow."

Daddy shifted her a little in his lap. ""I have an idea. I'm going to lend you my watch." He took if off his wrist and showed it to Annie. "You remember how to tell time. See, it's 10:30 right now. I want you to be home when both hands are at the twelve, when the noon whistle blows. That's an hour and a half. Will that be long enough for you?"

Annie nodded and wiped the tears off her cheeks with the back of her hand.

"I'll tell Mama that you have the watch and will return when both hands are on the twelve. It's important you be responsible about this. Mama and I will be trusting you to come back on time."

"I will."

Daddy tucked the watch into the front pocket of her overalls and kissed her. "Have a good visit with your tree." He set her down and went back into the shed. Annie could hear him moving things around inside.

She started up the path into the woods. It felt funny to wear her overalls again, especially since they hadn't been washed. She remembered the feel of the dead, wet kittens in her pockets and felt sad. Then she remembered the feel of Dusty and Buttercup tucked together in her front pocket where the watch was now. She realized how much they had grown while they were at Grandma's house. They wouldn't both fit in that pocket now.

As she neared the fort, Annie heard smashing sounds. She stopped at a bend in the path and peered around a bush. Donny was in the fort, standing up and knocking down the rocks that formed the wall. He was kicking them down, bending and pushing them, sometimes picking them up and throwing them. He was crying.

Annie stepped back. She was sad for Donny. She knew he didn't want to go to Boston and leave his friend. He'd be mad if she saw him crying. She retreated down the path a little way and went into the bushes on one side. The bushes were thick and scratchy, but Annie knew how to move through them, and she had both hands free now. She wasn't carrying kittens this time.

Misty and the kittens were safe in their cage, tucked behind the shed in the shade where they wouldn't be in danger from the movers. Daddy had said he'd keep an eye on them.

She moved carefully, pushing the branches aside, sometimes crawling on hands and knees to go through thick parts. When the smashing sounds were far behind her, she headed back to the path. It was easy to see now. Donny and Jack and Jack's daddy and her daddy had all gone up and down it. She hoped they hadn't scared the deer. She really wanted to see the deer again.

She came to the old log with the ferns growing out of it and stopped to peer again into the dark crack. It smelt moist and earthy. Probably it wasn't an entrance to the elf kingdom after all.

But the woods still felt magical to her. She tilted her head back and looked up into the leaves above with sunlight dancing through them and the blue sky beyond them so near and so far. She hoped there would be woods near her new home. She brushed her hand through the ferns and went on up the path.

The little clearing was empty. She stopped at its edge. The deer weren't there, but as she tilted her head back, she saw that the squirrel was. He looked down at her from a high branch, rippling his tail, then whisked around out of sight on the other side of the tree.

She gazed into the little clearing. She wanted to remember just how it looked. She loved the way the bushes and trees were all around it, making it like a safe nest in the middle of the woods, the way the grass bent in the breeze. She wanted to lie down in the grass and look at the trees and sky again, but she had to be back on time. So she crossed the clearing, pushed through the bushes that the deer had jumped over, and went on up the path.

It felt different now. She was older. She'd been only four when she found the path the first time. She was five now, and Daddy had given her his watch and trusted her to be responsible.

She came to the open space, climbed up to the cliff, and found her tunnel in the underbrush. Standing on the ledge, she looked down at the roof of her house and remembered how scared she'd been of Mama, so scared she couldn't go home. She remembered the night she'd stayed up in the woods—starlight and moon shadows and the fox and the raccoon and the owl. With a shiver, she remembered the diving shadow of the owl and the sudden blow and pain in her shoulder.

It already felt like long ago, like a dream. The owl scratch was better now. It only hurt a little when she moved certain ways. She was still scared of Mama sometimes, but she was bigger now and brave and strong and knew how to duck.

She crawled under the tree and sat down by the kittens' grave. She remembered each kitten, Dapple, Smokey, and Tiger, each one's special colors, and grieved anew that they were gone, buried, and she'd never see them grow up. She did not cry, but her heart hurt with a bad ache that got all mixed up with the ache from the black hole that the magic elf doctor couldn't fix.

After a while, she stirred, gathered up the faded flowers, and crawled back out to the ledge. There she found fresh flowers and leaves for Dapple, took them back to the grave, and arranged them around the rock with the mica in it.

At the mouth of the cave, she found the trowel and her stick. She went into the cave and lay down for a while, curled up, the way she had when she'd first found the cave. Then she went to the trunk of the spruce tree and leaned against it the way she'd wanted to before she left with Daddy.

She remembered when they were camping that Daddy said they should leave everything just as they found it, so she crawled all around the circle under the tree and smoothed out the needles and took her stick back and put it under the tree that it came from.

Daddy's watch ticked in her pocket. She pulled it out. The big hand was already at the eight. She'd have to start back.

One last time she stood on the cliff and looked down. She could see the roof of her house and the big moving truck in the driveway, the town with the school where she was going to go to kindergarten but now she wasn't, the factory with the dark blue-gray smoke coming out. Wind came up from the valley and ruffled her curls.

Time to go. With the trowel in her hand, one last time she backed down the tunnel in the underbrush and came out at the bottom of the cliff. Then … oh! The mama deer and her two young ones were in the open space, at the bottom where the woods started again. The mama was stretching her neck up to eat leaves off the lower branches of a tree, and the young ones were wandering near her, nibbling the grass.

She stilled, her heart lifting in delight. The mama deer turned her head and looked at Annie, gazing right into her eyes as she had done before. Then, after a moment, she turned back to eating leaves.

Annie stayed still, watching the deer as they moved around finding new green things to nibble on. She loved the soft brown of their fur, their long thin legs that could jump so magically, their beautiful big ears, the graceful movement of their necks.

It was hard to leave them, but she knew she must keep going. She pulled out the watch. The big hand was at the ten now. Moving slowly so as not to frighten the deer, she went down the steep open space and into the path through the woods. Donny wasn't at the fort anymore. The fort was gone, all the rocks scattered.

When she got back to the house, big men were carrying out the beds and the couch and the chairs and table and all the boxes and putting them in the truck. She gave Daddy the trowel and his watch and he was proud of her that she came back on time. Mama had a picnic ready, and they ate in the shade of the big tree that grew by Annie's window.

Meg sighed as her body softened into the car seat. Outside the window, the fields and woods of northern New Jersey flowed past. They had done it! The house in Woodsborough was empty and already miles behind them. Jesse was beside her, his hands easy on the wheel. The children were settled in the back seat, Donny absorbed in a pile of comic books that Jack had given him, and Annie talking softly to Misty.

Meg reached over and touched Jesse's thigh. "We did it," she said. "We are actually out of there."

"We sure are." He turned his head and smiled at her.

Meg smiled back and felt another level of tension dissolve. Four or five more hours of driving, one last night in the hotel, and tomorrow they would meet the moving truck at their new home and begin settling in. It seemed hard to believe that at last things were working out. What a wild week it had been. She felt as if she were waking from a bad dream.

There had been one point that morning when Meg had feared she wouldn't be able to keep her promise. They had gotten up early and started out from the farm before seven, leaving Jesse's brother, Don, to supervise the loading of the possessions they had stored there. In the Woodsborough house, there was still so much packing to be done, and the children were restless and underfoot. Jesse gave Donny permission to go to his fort.

When Annie had insisted she had to go to her cave, and kept insisting while Meg was trying to sort all the bathroom detritus, Meg had felt near the breaking point. But she hadn't raised her hand. The packing did go better with the children gone, and Annie did come back at noon as she promised. So it had been all right after all.

Meg felt a rush of sureness and strength go through her as she realized she had held back her temper in that moment of overwhelm. She hadn't even started to raise her hand. She let out a long, shuddering sigh. She *could* keep her promise. It would be different now. She never would strike her children again.

A shiver ran through her as she remembered how Annie had lifted her chin as she demanded to go to her cave. That was a new gesture for Annie. Jesse was right. Her night in the woods had changed her. Meg felt considerable trepidation about how she would deal with this new Annie, but it wouldn't be with violence. She also realized she was proud of Annie for standing up to her. Annie would grow up to be a strong woman.

And it seemed she had forgiven, or at least accepted, Meg again. She had come into Meg's arms, she had let Meg touch her kittens, and she had asked for the "Night" poem. That was such an immense relief Meg could still hardly believe it. She wondered what had happened to soften Annie during the two days she had been at the farm. Maybe Annie would tell her sometime. Maybe Meg would never know.

She turned in her seat to look back at Annie. She was holding Misty in her lap and stroking her. The cage with the kittens in it was open on the seat beside her.

"How's Misty doing?" Meg asked.

"Pretty well. She doesn't like riding in the car, but she's settling down now. She'll be glad when we get to our new house."

"We all will be," Meg said. Her heart ached with love. How incredibly sweet Annie was with her soft curls, her wide blue eyes, and the tender way she was cradling her kitty. "Would you like to come up front and ride in my lap for a while?"

Annie hesitated, frowning a little. "I think I need to stay here with Misty."

"Okay." Meg turned around again, disappointed. But it will be all right, she told herself. She has accepted me again. She's probably right to stay with Misty a while longer.

☙ ❧

Annie gathered Misty closer. Her chest was aching again. Misty's purring warmth made it feel better.

Mama had put a couple of pillows in the back seat, one for Donny and one for Annie. Donny had propped his against the side of the car and was leaning on it as he read his comic books. He was quiet, not paying any attention to Annie.

Annie pushed her pillow up against the side of the kittens' cage and leaned her head against it. The hole in her heart was hurting a lot. She held Misty closer and closed her eyes. She imagined the magic elf doctor sitting on the top of the cage. "I've covered the hole all up," he told her. "No one will know. Just forget it now. Then it won't hurt so much."

Could she forget it? She didn't know.

Mama wanted Annie to sit in her lap. She was being gentle. She had smiled at Annie and had that love look in her eyes. Maybe it would be okay. Daddy was right there.

Annie longed to be held by gentle Mama. She wanted to sit in Mama's lap. Maybe, she thought, I can sit in her lap and like it when

Mama is gentle and just watch out and get away when she changes. She won't do anything now with Daddy right beside us.

Annie let out a long, shuddering sigh. For a minute she felt like crying. But, no. She had to be brave like Daddy said.

She lifted her head. Misty wriggled in her arms. Annie had been holding her too tight. She let go. Misty stretched, then padded across Annie's lap and into the cage with her kittens. Annie watched as she licked them and lay down to nurse them.

"Mama," Annie said.

Mama turned around.

"Misty's nursing her babies. I can come sit in your lap now."

Mama smiled and held out her arms. "Come then."

Annie climbed over the seat and snuggled into Mama's lap. She fit just right and it felt so good to have Mama hold her. Mama kissed the top of her head. She was being really gentle.

Daddy started to sing. "Row, row, row your boat—"

It was a round. Annie loved rounds and the way Mama's and Daddy's voices fit together even though they were singing different parts of the song. Mama joined in, singing "Row, row, row your boat" while Daddy sang "Gently down the stream." Then Donny joined in. Annie knew the song, too, but she didn't sing.

She nestled in Mama's arms, feeling the song and Mama's breath moving in Mama's chest, feeling Daddy close beside them, hearing Donny singing from the back seat. The car hummed under her, carrying them all together to their new home, and the song swirled around her, easing the ache in her heart.

"Merrily, merrily, merrily,
Life is but a dream."

About the Author

Heather Starsong grew up in New England and graduated summa cum laude from Boston University in 1957 with a Bachelor of Arts in Comparative Literature.

She has been a dancer since childhood, especially fascinated with the connections between healing, art, and spirit. She has explored and taught many forms: creative dance, liturgical dance, dance therapy, yoga, ceremonial dance, Rolfing® and Rolf Movement,® Continuum, and most recently Argentine Tango.

Although her career has been focused on body language, she has loved and told stories all her life. In 2007 she began to write her stories. *Leaves in Her Hair* was published in 2009, *Never Again* in 2015, *The Purest Gold* in 2017, and *Song of Eliria* in 2019.

She is presently semi-retired from a long career of teaching dance and yoga and practicing Rolfing. She lives in Boulder, Colorado, and enjoys writing, dancing, hiking in the high country, and spending time with her grandchildren.

Find out more about Heather Starsong on her web page: www.heatherstarsong.com

Also from Heather Starsong

Never Again

Leaves in Her Hair

The Purest Gold

Song of Eliria

www.heatherstarsong.com

www.ingramcontent.com/pod-product-compliance
Lightning Source LLC
Chambersburg PA
CBHW030436010526
44118CB00011B/664